The
Church
Revitalization
Playbook

Ed Trinkle

Thank you Father in heaven, for showing me and our church's that "Nothing is impossible with God."

Thank you to my beautiful wife, Kimberly and our daughters, Kristina, Katie, Kelsea, and Emily, for walking with me faithfully to everywhere God has called us!

The Church Revitalization Playbook

Ed Trinkle

The Church Revitalization Playbook by Ed Trinkle
Copyright © 2021 by Ed Trinkle
All Rights Reserved.
ISBN: 978-1-59755-653-8
Published by: ADVANTAGE BOOKS™
                   www.advboostore.com

Unless otherwise indicated Scripture quotations are taken from THE HOLY BIBLE, NEW INTERNATIONAL VERSION®. Copyright© 1973, 1978, 1984, 2011 by Biblica, Inc.™. Used by permission of Zondervan

Scriptures marked (ESV) are taken from the THE HOLY BIBLE, ENGLISH STANDARD VERSION® Copyright© 2001 by Crossway, a publishing ministry of Good News Publishers. Used by permission.

Scripture quotations marked "ASV" are taken from the American Standard Version Bible (Public Domain).

LIBRARY OF CONGRESS CONTROL NUMBER: 2021943352
NAME: Trinkle, Ed, Author
TITLE: The Church Revitalization Playbook / Ed Trinkle
               Advantage Books, 2021
IDENTIFIERS: 9781597556538 (print)
               9781597556587 (eBook)
SUBJECTS: RELIGION: Christian Church – Growth
               RELIGION: Christian Living – Leadership & Mentoring

First Printing: AUGUST 2021
21 22 23 24 25 26   10 9 8 7 6 5 4 3 2 1

ENDORSEMENTS

DR. GENE GETZ, host and teacher of *Renewal Radio*, has been a Senior Pastor, Professor, and author of more than 60 books. He has been a church-planting pastor in the Dallas Metroplex since 1972 and has served as an adjunct professor at *Dallas Theological Seminary*. Gene is President of the Center for Church Renewal and serves as Pastor Emeritus of *Chase Oaks Church* (formerly *Fellowship Bible Church North*) in Plano, Texas.

One of his books, THE MEASURE OF A MAN, has sold more than a *million* copies. Dr. Getz says:

"As lead and support pastors we all need encouragement in difficult situations. Ed Trinkle offers this encouragement. He writes out of experience. He has helped renew several churches that were on 'life support' for various reasons, including financial irresponsibility, sexual immorality and general incompetence in the leadership. Ed also addresses leadership successes, church discipline, and church structure."

CRAIG JOHNSON is the Executive Pastor at Joel's Osteen's *Lakewood Church* in Houston, Texas, and the founder of CHAMPIONS CLUBS. He says:

"Ed Trinkle is one of the most amazing pastors I know. Anyone who can navigate the most difficult church transitions and do it with grace like Ed does is truly special. He is an exceptional leader. In Church Revitalization Playbook Ed will help any pastor who is called to turn a complicated and big ship from barely making it to a streamlined church organization. He's one of the best I've ever seen. I could not give a higher recommendation and more praise for Church Revitalization Playbook and I know if you will follow his blue print in how to navigate the most difficult situations you will come out on the other side with a strong church and has an even better leader."

ANTHONY MILAS is the Lead Pastor of Granite United Church in Salem, New Hampshire.

I have known Ed Trinkle for more than 40 years, since we were young teenagers spending our days playing basketball, football, hitting the beach, and figuring life out one day at a time. The thing about Ed was that even as a teenager Ed was gifted with the incredible gift of leadership. It didn't matter where Ed was he always gathered a crowd around him and led the way. Ed is a PROBLEM SLOVER. He doesn't look at any situation with the attitude of "what we don't have," but always with a "here's what we've got and we'll move forward from here." What I didn't realize was how this attitude would play into GOD leading Ed into CHURCH REVITALIZATION MINISTRY. I have watched Ed step into incredibly messy situations and take the high road without finding fault in how a ministry got to where it was. Ed has been used of GOD to breathe life back into dead churches, he has been used to bring back hope to hurting church families, and he has brought honor back to the BRIDE OF CHRIST. I have seen him lead broken church out of millions of dollars of debt to become debt free and healthy. I have seen Ed lead churches that were once at the brink of closing their doors become thriving congregations once again. If you are looking for a coach or resource that is personable, passionate, and proven, look no further. THE CHURCH REVITALIZATION BOOK is for you.

Table of Contents

Ed Trinkle

Chapter 1

Time of Death

The final episode of the highly successful Emmy-winning television series, M.A.S.H. (an acronym for Mobile Army Surgical Hospital) aired way back in 1983. But reruns still play several times a day somewhere on cable. The "police action" in Korea of President Harry Truman lasted only three years, but the comedy-drama involving the antics of Hawkeye, Radar, Klinger, and company lasted for twelve. Each episode featured an odd convergence of belly laughs and heart-wrenching drama, all part of life in the unit bearing the number 4077.

Even the oldest members of the "Millennial Generation" are too young to remember the show's finale, "Goodbye, Farewell and Amen," a cultural event that transcended its medium and remained the most watched television episode for more than 25 years. I still enjoy the reruns. I certainly don't mean to trivialize the stark reality of war—especially to anyone who has actually been there or has had loved ones in harm's way—but when I was a kid, watching M.A.S.H. made war somehow seem real to me for the first time. I recently re-watched an episode about a severely wounded soldier. He had been airlifted to the 4077th by one of the iconic M.A.S.H. helicopters, but by the time he was rushed into surgery, he was brain-dead.

And it was Christmas Day.

The doctors were determined to keep his body alive long enough so that his death certificate would not show him dying on Christmas. But they came up short. With about an hour to go on December 25th, his body could survive no longer. Doctor Benjamin Franklin "Hawkeye" Pierce made the decision to turn the clock forward so that he could say, "Time of death, 12:05 a.m., December 26th." Though not actually the truth, it was understandable.

Now, I had watched this episode many times, but this time I found myself thinking, does it really matter when the actual time of death was, if he was dead anyway? Then the answer hit me—that was the moment when all efforts to revive the body ceased. It was over. It was time to clean up and move on to the next patient.

I wonder how many ministry leaders have tried everything they can think of but still struggle with making a "time of death" declaration when it comes to their particular local church. Not to belabor the television illustrations, but it makes me think of those defibrillators doctor's use. My kids would call them "shocky-paddles." It seems like every episode of a TV hospital drama includes a scene where those things are charged up and the doctor yells "Clear!" before zapping someone's chest in an attempt to bring them back from the brink of death.

It got me to thinking: Are there "shocky-paddles" for ministries? Is it ever okay to cease life-saving efforts and call "time of death" for a local church?

If so—when?

A few years ago, I read a great book by Thom Rainer titled, *Autopsy of a Deceased Church*. The last section of the book contained three chapters answering the question, "Is there hope for a dying church?" He wrote about the symptoms of a sick church, with one chapter actually titled, My Church is Dying. One of the problems in a dying church is how to determine time of death. It is an understandably difficult and painful call for church leaders.

When you feel sick and decide to seek medical attention, the first part of the process is diagnosis. You cannot treat what cannot be identified. Sometimes the diagnosis is bad. Sadly, sometimes it is even fatal. Frankly, to actually diagnose church death is painful, an admission that things have digressed to the point of hopelessness. And it can't be fixed. One important thing to remember is this: The church was never really ours. Sure, we casually talk about "our" church like it is part of our family lineage or bloodline. But that is not completely correct.

A few years ago, my daughters gave me one of those DNA test kits so I could trace my ancestry. I loved it and was fascinated to be able to trace my family tree to Western Europe. If you have been connected to the same church for more than one generation, you are certainly blessed with a great church ancestry. It is your spiritual home and probably very special to you. You have likely made significant spiritual decisions there, maybe it is where you were married, maybe you have raised your children in that church, and maybe you have said goodbye to dear friends and family at church funerals. A church like that becomes part of the fabric of your life, like a close family member. And you look beyond flaws and shortcomings because you love it too much to become fixated on anything bad. To ever admit that "our" church is sick, or even dying, well, we usually prefer to live in denial.

But was it ever really our church?

I do it, too. I refer to the church as "ours" or "mine" in a personal, sometimes even possessive way. But I do so in a familial way. But again, the truth is the church is never really "ours" or "mine." The Church is the Bride of Christ. He gave himself for it. It belongs to Him. He started it. He paid for it. He sustains it.

Of course, we make a distinction between a particular local church body and the universal family of God composed of anyone who has confessed Jesus Christ as Lord and Savior. The local church is the visible ekklesia, a called-out body of believers tasked with ministering in and to a particular community, reaching people with the life changing gospel of Jesus Christ. I currently lead such a ministry in Plano, Texas, called Warehouse Church. I love it and live for it, because when you are part of a local church for a long time, it becomes part of you and you become part of it.

The problem with this is that local churches can tend to become like the people, instead of the people becoming more and more like the Bridegroom—Christ Himself. The more a church is defined by the characteristics of its imperfect and fallen members, the more it puts church health at risk. This is an ominous early step on the slippery slope that leads to church death.

About a decade ago, a sermon series called *No Perfect People Allowed* was popular in many American churches. The series was based on a great book with that title written by John Burke. I loved the book, and I have preached that series at every church I have pastored. I am a big proponent of the church being a place of grace, forgiveness, restoration, prayer, and new life. We must embrace imperfect people like ourselves and do whatever it takes to get them to the feet of Jesus. But what happens when your church, the church you love, the church where you are a member, the church you have given generously to, takes on the traits of its imperfect people? What happens when your church is not healthy? What happens when your church is "living in sin?" What happens when your church has a reputation for lying, being untrustworthy, or even immoral? What happens when the church takes more than it gives? What happens when the church has lost its way? What happens when your church is dead, and nobody knows it or will admit it?

How would the time of death be determined? Maybe you could look back and identify some major mistakes church leaders have made so you can pinpoint it historically. After all, we work better with facts than we do with theory. No one would argue that if you were to jump off a 100-story building you would die. The time or cause of death would not be debated. What we debate are things that cause slow death. For example, smoking, eating too much sugar, not eating enough healthy food, and never exercising can lead to poor health and eventual death.

But there are other things that tend to lead to slow death, variables like DNA, family history, weather, the Farmer's Almanac, and so forth. We have the tendency to need a scapegoat when things are going wrong. And the local church is infamous for being a place where people get hurt, pastors mess up, boards operate out of control, and members lose their way. When these things occur, we tend to look for ways to spread the blame around.

How would you determine the time of death for a local church? After all, with the human body there are vital signs used as key indicators, things like temperature, pulse rate, respiration rate, and blood pressure. And there is another way the time of death is determined, particularly by a forensic investigator. They use insects, from blow flies to beetles. There is a whole discipline called Forensic Entomology. It is the study of insects for medical purposes pertaining to death. As a human corpse goes through stages of decay, bugs can help determine when the body started to decompose.

It begs the question: are there stages of decay for the church that has already died?

Wrong Ways to Determine Time of Death

We do not dare to classify or compare ourselves with some who commend themselves. When they measure themselves by themselves and compare themselves with themselves, they are not wise. – II Corinthians 10:12

We need to guard against COMPARISON. We compare numbers, facilities, "coolness" factors, lead pastors, energy levels, styles of worship, children's programs, missionary outreach programs and so on. The Apostle Paul simply tells us, "do not compare yourself to anyone." If your church membership/attendance is 120 and you compare it to a church of 6000, you will feel very small, if not dead. But the truth is that not every church running in the thousands is vibrant and healthy. The opposite is also true, just because a church runs 120 on Sunday does not mean it is dead.

This is not to say numbers are not important. They represent people, and God has called us to reach people—the life-blood of a church growing organically. An organism that shows no growth or signs of life is dead. The problem with comparison is that no two churches are exactly alike. God has distributed gifts according to His sovereign will. The church that runs in the thousands may be great on evangelism but could stand some improvement on discipleship, and vice versa for the smaller church. Our only comparison ought to be with Jesus Christ, as Paul wrote in Philippians 2:5: *"Let this mind be in you which was also in Christ Jesus."*

We should also be careful not to measure the health of a church by its financial balance sheet or assets. Some of the largest church campuses are in the Dallas-Fort Worth Metroplex. Does this mean that every such church is truly heathy? I am certainly not saying they are not, but does the size of a building and abundant finances indicate church health?

Another area for caution in determining the time of church death is when analyzing a congregation's age demographic with the idea that an older median age means a church is dying. This judgment falls into the category of observing surface statistics. Young Christians are not inherently better Christians than older ones. Frankly, the younger need the wisdom of the older, and the older need the vitality of the younger. Heathy churches tend to be effectively inter-generational.

Another faulty indicator is when a pastor or other key leader makes significant mistakes. This can be tough. There are ways a leader can absolutely disqualify himself or herself. But we throw the term disqualify around rather carelessly, at times—as if we are the qualifying arbiters for the church. While there are mistakes that clearly forfeit the ability of a leader to lead, we can develop an unhealthy appetite for sordid and sensationalized stories that can lead to knee-jerk decisions.

Determining TIME of DEATH

There are physical, emotional, and spiritual factors in the death of a local church. To determine if a church is dying, consider this very general statement: Growth is the evidence of life—without it, a church is either dying or dead.

A church can display signs of life by people being brought to faith in Christ through outreach. A while back, I talked to a pastor who served in the rural outskirts of Fort Worth, Texas. He was discouraged because only 15 people were converted the previous year. I talked to another pastor who reported 100 additions to his church during the same period. If you look deeper, you will notice that the first church—the one with just 15 conversions—grew from 30 to 45 in attendance—that's factor of 50%. While the other church—the one that had 100 additions—already had 1,000 in attendance, so grew only 10%. The smaller church actually showed more signs of life.

A church that "contracts" over the course of a year may not actually be dying; it may be pruning for future growth. Signs of life need to be measured over the long-term. Another evidence of life is this—do the members still love their church and do they support its leadership? I have pastored churches where I did not like what we were doing, or where we were going. I knew we had plenty of work to do and a long way to go, but in all honesty, I did not want to invite people to the church in its current state. When leaders and congregants love their church enough to invite others to attend, that is a huge proof of life. To invite others to a church that is dying is akin to doing a mailer to advertise a funeral for someone people have never met. We want to bring people to something fun, exciting, and growing. In other words—a church that evidences proof of life.

Physical death is also evident when the church is not regenerating itself. Can you count weeks, months, or even years since your church has had people saved and baptized in the services? If the church is not regularly regenerating and replenishing itself, it is on a fast track to being a single generation church.

Other indicators of looming church death would include run-down properties, chronic financial problems, vanishing programs, and very little activity strangled by a rigid services schedule. Would your community miss your church if it were to close? If not, it may be time to call the time of death.

Emotional death has to do with the wants, likes, and dislikes of the church. For instance, emotional death takes place when we love the things that make us feel good in the church, while demonstrating no compassion for the needs of the larger community. It reminds me of that hit song from years ago, sung by the Righteous Brothers—*You've Lost that Lovin' Feelin'*—we find ourselves doing everything out of duty, almost out of muscle memory. But with no real heart or passion.

Emotional death happens when congregants want church to be about them when it should be about God and others. When I talk to church leaders about this, I like to ask a lot of WHY questions.

- Why do we do things the way we do?

- Why do we have the music we have?

- Why do we do the services the way we do them?

- Why do people come to our church?

- Why don't we have more guests in our church?

The answers to these questions are very telling. They can reveal signs of life, or they can help to determine the time of death.

Sometimes spiritual death is a result of something deep and damaging, when a church has generational sins that have never been confronted. God has removed his anointing and glory—a case of Ichabod.

Spiritual death can also be evident when the internal mission of the church is no longer tied to God's purpose for the church. Dead and dying churches often have a lot of angry people. They have a condescending attitude to everyone else and elevate themselves as more "spiritual" than others. They are like the church at Ephesus described in Revelation chapter 2—seeing themselves as doing well, when in fact they are very sick. When this kind of thing is predominant in the congregation, the pronouncement of time of death is not too far behind.

The three areas we've covered, physical, emotional, and spiritual health and death, often occur simultaneously, making the time of death relatively easy to recognize. But I think a church can recover from physical and emotional death with a serious plan for revitalization.

The great news is that Jesus is the architect of RESURRECTION. John 11:25 tells us, *"Jesus said to her, 'I am the resurrection and the life. He who believes in Me, though he may die, he shall live.'"*

Ed Trinkle

Chapter 2

Resurrection Blues?

The very idea of a resurrection was controversial, even a little scary, during the time when Jesus walked on the earth. It's exciting for us to think about the coming final resurrection, but it's something no one has yet experienced. A couple of prominent Jewish religious groups actually separated over the issue of resurrection—one believed in it, the other did not. But they put aside those differences when it came to hating Jesus—the architect of resurrection. He demonstrated resurrection power when he brought his friend Lazarus back from the dead, as recorded in John chapter eleven. And a closer look at that story will help us understand just how the issue of church revitalization is, in fact, about resurrection.

Jesus knew what He was doing

Jesus was about two miles away from Lazarus the moment he died—about an hour's walk. He had been very close to Lazarus, as well as his sisters, Mary and Martha. They were likely around the same age as Jesus—at least age-range—and were good friends. Lazarus's death was certainly difficult for his sisters to accept. Not only was their brother young, but he was a close friend to the Great Physician—the one who went everywhere healing the sick. Three people confronted Jesus about showing up too late. They were mourning because their brother died and the one who could have helped Lazarus had been absent. They questioned Jesus's tardiness, while acknowledging their belief in His healing power. "If only you had been here," they lamented.

If only...

Throughout this book I will refer to three churches I have pastored. I served University Church in Jacksonville, Florida from 2002-2008. Then I pastored what would eventually become The Bridge Church near Philadelphia, Pa, from 2008-2015. And since 2015, I have led The Warehouse Church in Plano Texas.

University Church was a Revitalization Project, while The Bridge Church and The Warehouse Church are replants, or as I will refer to them, Resurrection Projects. When my wife and I moved to North Dallas in 2015, we were called to take over an unhealthy church that was in a very delicate situation. Canyon Creek Baptist Church had been in existence for 42 years at the time we took over. Three of the last four pastors had moral failures. The church had enormous debt in proportion to its size. There were too many buildings to manage, and it operated a Christian school that was dysfunctional and debt-ridden year after year. It was a financial albatross around the church's neck, driving the total debt to more than seven million dollars.

God has given my wife and me a huge burden for Church Revitalization and Resurrection. We hope to use our experiences with these three churches to help other churches experience their own breakthroughs. I remember when I was being interviewed by Canyon Creek Baptist Church, one of the members said, "it's been such a long time since we felt the presence of the Lord here." This reminded me of the three people in Lazarus's story who scolded, "if you had only been here, he would still be alive." He told them that resurrection had arrived.

Jesus came to demonstrate His power

When you read the story, you see how deeply Jesus cared for Lazarus. He raised his friend from the dead. Lazarus was not in a coma, or "mostly dead," or brain-dead, he was dead-dead. He had been in a tomb for a few days. When Jesus instructed men to roll the covering stone away, the King James Version graphically described Lazarus's condition, "He stinketh."

If I were a pessimist, I might use the same language to describe the ministry situations we inherited, they "stinketh." What we had to clean up in Philly and in North Dallas really did stink! People were hurting, faithful and kind people who had lost their confidence in leadership, and with that their passion for reaching people. The egregious moral and financial leadership failures caused the people to feel as if God had abandoned them. They prayed earnestly and fervently. And they called us as an expression of hope for revitalization, not fully understanding the severity and gravity of their situation.

When I was interviewed in Texas, a member asked if I would stay if we sold the property and had to start meeting in a rented facility, would I stay? The property was 180,000 square feet, with a colonial style worship center and a very liturgical looking, dated facility. My response turned out to be prophetic. I said, "Yes, sir. I will stay and see the church through the move. Will you?" He did not. As a matter of fact, of the 180 people voting for us in April 2015, only 18 are in the church today.

It is not mere optimism to suggest that Lazarus's death had always been part of God's plan to demonstrate His power over life and death, for God to be glorified, and people to believe that God sent Jesus to do a great work (*"that they may believe You sent Me"* – John 11:42).

Lazarus had to die.

To call the time of death for a church, to actually come to the realization that someone has failed, or a group of people have failed, and the church has lost its ability to influence the community is a gut-punch. To suggest that it was part of the masterplan all along is, however, something of a head-scratcher. God wanted Lazarus to die? He was okay with Mary and Martha suffering emotionally? He was okay with Lazarus being dead long enough to decompose? I believe the answer to all of these questions is an unqualified, yes.

God wanted to prove through Jesus's power, that Jesus was God's Son. I also wonder if people left disappointed because Jesus did not show up. Probably so. Lazarus's death was surrounded by disappointment. I believe there was disappointment when Canyon Creek Baptist Church died. I cannot lie, some of the people who left were people we knew had to go. But for many, it was hard.

It is very difficult to shut off the care chamber in our heart when we love someone.

Many of the people who left had something that I describe as, "Canyon Fatigue." Some of the people left loud and ugly. They were hurt and they reacted. On some level, I knew they weren't mad at me, but it didn't always feel that way. In Lazarus's story, Mary was upset, Martha was, too, and so were the people surrounding them. But Jesus was not surprised, because He came to demonstrate the power of God.

For Miracle witnesses, a resurrection is really hard to believe

The first recorded person in the Bible to believe in resurrection was Abraham. When Abraham took his son Isaac to Mount Moriah to sacrifice him in obedience to what God told him to do, God actually performed an easier miracle than Abraham was expecting. Abraham believed God wanted him to sacrifice his son, but Abraham also believed that God was going to raise him from the dead. The easier miracle was that God provided a sacrifice and spared Abraham the heartache of killing his only son. It is a beautiful picture of God's love, because God did not ask Abraham to do something that HE was not willing to do for us.

One interesting thing about Lazarus's resurrection was that when his sisters knew he was dead, they thought there was nothing that Jesus could do. But Jesus wanted to do a miracle even greater than healing his friend's disease. He wanted to bring him back to life. Mary, Martha, the crowd and the disciples, experienced shock and awe, but should they have been so amazed? They had seen several of their Lord's significant miracles. Lazarus was not even Jesus's first resurrection, but they did not think this was a possibility in Lazarus's case.

So, this begs a difficult question about Canyon Creek Baptist Church. Did God want it to die? When the church was birthed in the early 1970s, every person reached, every big attendance day, every building built, and every financial victory was known by God. And He also knew that on June 30, 2017, the existence of Canyon Creek Baptist Church, would be no more. In eternity past, God knew the start and end dates of the church.

And he also knew the first day for The Warehouse Church.

We can all relate to Mary, Martha, the disciples, and the crowd for being afraid. Calling the time of death for Canyon Creek was very difficult—even surreal. I had been the pastor for just over two years when we made this call. We prayed, and we knew it was right, but we also knew this was not just the end of a sad story.

It was the beginning of a new one.

The greatest resurrection story in the Bible, of course, is not about Lazarus, but of Jesus. Jesus's cruel death had to happen in order for God's power to be fully demonstrated through His resurrection. His death brought forth life. The death of a church does not have to be final; it can be the start of something exciting and new. There is life after death.

God has a wonderful plan for your life—and your church. He already knows our appointed time, because it is appointed unto man once to die. God knows the shelf-life of relevancy and health for your church. Your church may need a heart transplant, those "shocky paddles," or a complete resurrection. Think about this, if that's what it will take to bring your church to its greatest days of ministry, its greatest harvest, it greatest community impact, would you agree to it?

God loves His Church more than we do. God loved Lazarus more than his friends or sisters did. The scriptures do not give us a Lazarus "follow-up" interview—a post-post mortem. But, I wonder what his answer would have been to this question: "Lazarus, did you want to come back?" This is just a guess, but I think his answer might very well have been, NO!

You may have great reasons to love your church, but no matter what your church may mean to you, you did not have to die to pay for its existence. Jesus did.

God has a plan that is far greater than we can comprehend. The plan to draw people to Him, post Lazarus's resurrection, was sheer genius. Who among those who saw such a huge miracle could turn away in disbelief? God wants to demonstrate His power through us and His church, but in order to do this, we must be spiritually alive.

As a result of the death of Canyon Creek Baptist Church, over 1.4 Million dollars were given to missionaries and church planters worldwide. That means, because the church "died," ten missionaries received desperately needed new vehicles for their ministries, two bible colleges were given a lifeline, and two orphanages were started. God used death to fuel life.

The Warehouse Church began July 1, 2017, with an average weekly attendance of 94 in its first month. By November 2018, attendance hit 400 for the first time, and on that Christmas weekend, 532 attended.

God's way is always the best way. Lazarus could have been healed before he died instead of needing resurrection. That would have made his loved ones very happy. But Jesus chose to give them more of a "WOW" factor. God's plan for our church was that it had to die. Such a death might have been avoidable 10-15 years earlier, but for us in 2017, there was no other choice. And it was this choice that helped us to understand God's plan for our future.

The scriptures are silent on the subject of how much longer Lazarus lived after his resurrection encounter with Jesus. But it is clear that after his resurrection more people believed Jesus was who He said He was. Lazarus's resurrection by Jesus prepared His followers and the world for the next resurrection to come—His own. And the resurrection of Jesus would impact all of history and eternity.

Ed Trinkle

Chapter 3

A Tale of Four Cities

This chapter is dedicated to the faithful church families and leaders of University Church in Jacksonville, FL, led by Pastor Frank Ciresi, two churches in Pennsylvania, the combination of which is The Bridge Church in Linwood, PA, led by Pastor Aaron Harding, and Warehouse Church in Plano, TX where God has allowed me to lead since 2015. I have had the honor of serving at all three churches as lead pastor. In all of these churches I have worked with some very godly, wise, and generous board members. My goal in sharing the story of each church is to give God the glory for the work He did through some faithful people. One of the first principles I wrote about earlier was that the church belongs to God. He paid for it. Every accomplishment and testimony from these great churches is being shared to honor the Provider and Sustainer, our All-Powerful Jehovah God.

I want to be careful to share the purpose of describing this "tale of four cities." The emphasis is on the story, not the mistakes that lead to the demise. I am not a better pastor than the three I followed at each respective church. I have made plenty of personal and leadership mistakes. To list them would require a much bigger book. There are many factors that lead to each previous pastor leaving, but I believe the one thing that they all had in common was God's will and timing. I will share brief facts to paint a picture, but I will not mention any pastor or leader by name. I will be accurate with historical facts, some of which are difficult to talk about and were even harder to live through.

City Number One: JACKSONVILLE, FLORIDA

University Church was formerly known as University Baptist Church in Jacksonville, Florida. The name was derived from its location on University Boulevard. The church was started in the 1950s and was led for more than 50 years by a man who had been a mentor to Dr. Jerry Falwell. His name was Dr. Jack Dinsbeer. The church started a Christian School in 1970—one of the most well-known schools in Northeast Florida. They have a vigorous academic program, and an athletic department that has won state championships in wrestling, baseball, softball, and football. I am very blessed that two of my daughters graduated from UC (University Christian School), and all four of my girls were enrolled there for up to six years each.

My wife and I were called to University in January 2002. We did not directly follow Dr. Dinsbeer, but we followed another good man, Dr. Charles Davis. Dr. Davis, formerly of Trinity Baptist College in Jacksonville, was called to pastor University Baptist Church after Dr. Dinsbeer. Dr. Davis was there for two years. I had the privilege of leading the church for six years—2002-2008.

During the last few years of Dr. Dinsbeer's tenure, one of the workers in the finance department embezzled a large sum of money from the church. Dr. Dinsbeer personally covered a large portion of this loss and eventually resigned. Dr. Dinsbeer is still loved and revered by the church family and leaders of UC, and his resignation saddened the soul of the church. Dr. Davis came in and loved the church through the difficult transition. It is a very daunting task to follow an iconic leader. When the dust settled from the money controversy, Dr. Davis started to lead the church through a transition in methodology, but he resigned when resistance mounted. By then, the church was sick and broken.

When we arrived in 2002, my wife and I were young (37 years old) and brought some energy, as well as a plan to heal and grow the church. The church was broken not dead. We needed to do some physical things and tend to some emotional needs, but the core of the church was in recovery, and we were preparing to restore health.

The ministry was complicated. The Christian school was very large—nearly 1000 students, including a pre-school. The church owned a large tract of land, all of which needed attention. There was a campus church for the employees of the school. The main church sanctuary had a leaky roof, water-stained carpets, and there was a dank and musty smell. The sanctuary could hold about 500 people, yet there were only two tiny restrooms—and neither one was ADA-compliant.

Since the church had been through such a difficult time, the emphasis of the ministry became all about the school. The school staff needed "repair" from some of its own issues, and the lifeline of the ministry, the church, needed an overhaul. Pretty dire.

We put a multi-dimensional plan together. One thing was that we needed to deal with some inconsistencies in the church's by-laws. We also had to recruit and build a team to minister to the community. And we needed to get younger—fast. We needed to make church exciting and something to look forward to. We also needed people to come to the church who were not affiliated with the school. We had to find a way to bridge the gap between church and school. And we needed to restore confidence within the church body, confidence that the church had life and purpose.

When we introduced the first changes, we had some excitement and momentum. But as expected, we soon had resistance. Sometimes, when you hear stories of transitional speedbumps from other churches, they sound exaggerated, but this tale is not. University was a traditional church, with traditional values, conservative doctrine, and outdated methods. The congregation was very chronologically mature, yet spiritually stagnant. When you ask a congregation if they want to grow, they will usually respond yes, and when you ask if they are willing to do things differently, most will still say yes. But when we actually introduced and implemented change, we experienced significant resistance.

I encountered my first church "bully" before we even found a place to live in Jacksonville. I will refer to him as "Mr. Royal." Mr. Royal waited for me after church my first Sunday as the new pastor in Jacksonville. He wanted to take me out to lunch after church to "discuss my proposed plans." Some of the young families whispered in my ear, "get ready and be careful." He took me to a pretty fancy country club and asked me if I would be interested in joining, under his membership plan. He introduced to me to some pretty impressive people at his club. I met some bankers—even the owner of the Jacksonville Jaguars. Heady stuff.

Mr. Royal made a proposal to me that day, one that he assured me would guarantee church growth. He said he wanted to pay for a banner that was needed in front of the church, one that said, "Traditional Music and KJV Bible still loved at University!" Yikes!

I listened to the threat that followed, and was shocked, but in a strange way respected his candor. He said, "Ed, or would you prefer I call you, 'Pastor?'" He was my senior by 35 years, so I told him "anything you want Mr. Royal." He said if I did this for him and the seniors, the church would keep his $60,000 worth of annual giving, which he literally said, "represents your salary package." He then guaranteed that many disgruntled givers from all over Jacksonville would move their membership to our church. He was probably right. He spoke against the "Purpose Driven Church" movement, secularized church music, and the culture shift of casual dress on Sundays. I told him that I believed God wanted us to grow the church by reaching unchurched, unsaved families, that anyone was welcomed to University and that I would not be wearing a suit to church anymore. He tried his hardest to persuade me that day, and then once a week for the next three months with memorable e-mails and post-church conversations.

I remember that, toward the end of his time with us, he told me that the church could not afford to lose his tithe. I told him I loved him and was grateful for his years of serving at University but would not let him control the church. He eventually left the church, taking some other angry and disgruntled people with him.

The church grew at a steady pace, but not quickly. We finished the updated by-laws in our first year, then we put a plan together to refurbish the building, raising $250,000 to put new restrooms in the auditorium, adding new carpet and paint throughout the building, and updating the classrooms and lobby. I was able to hire a new team of young, enthusiastic staff members and began retiring and transitioning staff that needed to move on.

As the face of the congregation began to change toward young members, it was hard for many of the seniors. So, we spent extra time attending their class and social events in an effort to strengthen those relationships. We wanted them to know that the greatest way we could honor their legacy was not merely to preserve and protect it, but to pass it on. I learned so much about myself and other people during those first years. While there still were some dark secrets from past leadership that we would need to deal with down the road, the church was stabilizing and growing.

The biggest speedbump to our growth was all of the time and energy we had to spend on the school. I am not anti-school, per se, but I don't think I would ever be in a place where I would want to start a Christian school anywhere for any reason. My preference would be a board-run school formed from partnerships with a group of cooperative, non-controlling churches and business people. Nonetheless, University Christian School was a powerhouse. We had nearly 1,000 students and a pretty tight-knit community of more than 120 employees.

We had to work through some "staff infections" during our first two years, with significant turnover. We were sued a couple of times, but the litigation was never seriously threatening. We soon discovered that resistance was around the corner. We had to fire a prominent athletic coach, an action that brought negative attention. We were even called by the city's main sports radio morning program, and I was requested to speak on air about this firing. Thankfully the church stood behind us, and we plowed through.

After five years of church growth, personal maturing, and daily leadership lessons, the Lord grew our church back to more than 600 in Sunday attendance. We had two services on Sunday mornings, were able to refurbish the church facility, and we stabilized the church governance along with that of the Christian School. Yet, there was spiritual darkness to confront to get the church to a place of complete health. One of our early supporters turned on me and our leadership in our final year at the church. We were finishing some intense deacon's meetings, during which we were securing the church by-laws and changing some of our business practices, and after the meeting this deacon wanted to talk to me.

He was the second church bully we had to confront. We were outside of the church on a Wednesday night, and this deacon stood up to me. He started poking me in the chest, speaking about his frustration with the way he thought we were "secularizing" the church. He did not approve of the music, the transition to non-KJV Bible versions, and a litany of other things. I distinctly remember this confrontation because I wanted to knock his block off. The irony of his bullying is that I was taller than him by eight inches and probably twice his weight. It wouldn't have been a fair fight. I asked the Lord for strength after he poked me for the third time, because I wanted to punch his lights out. God was so gracious to me and gave me a word in response. God told me to tell him, "Whatever is going on in your life, you are not reacting to me, you are not mad at me, you are mad at personal life circumstances, how can I help you or pray for you?" He became infuriated and stormed off.

Two months after that confrontation, we had an active shooter situation on our campus on a Wednesday night. More than 20 gunshots were fired. Fortunately, no one was hurt except for the shooter. One month later, leaders from my home church in Philadelphia called and asked us to consider moving from Jacksonville and leading that congregation. Then in the same week, the deacon who had confronted me earlier was arrested for soliciting a male prostitute who turned out to be an under-cover police officer. It was revealed that he was a repeat offender with charges in two other states. We took these developments before the deacons and the church, and his tenure as a leader was finished, as was his marriage and family as he knew it. This was heartbreaking, but we thank God for great leaders who helped us navigate through this complicated set of circumstances.

My wife and I learned so many things about life and leadership in Jacksonville. We served with great leaders and staff. We had the privilege of hiring an executive pastor, whom we recommended to the church to call as lead pastor. Pastor Frank Ciresi was called and has been lead pastor since 2008. University Church is still a thriving vibrant church in the Southside area of the city of Jacksonville.

In Jacksonville, we learned how to diagnose the health of a church. We learned how to put a great team of leaders together to help formulate a plan to restore church health, while reaching new families with the Gospel of Jesus Christ. I learned how to say I was sorry when I made mistakes. We learned the health of the church would be restored because of and by the Great Physician. University was not dead, it was simply sick. God restored physical and emotional health to this church. Probably our greatest achievement was simple obedience to the Lord's calling and greater submission to His leadership. I learned many lessons about personal growth from great deacons and committed team members. One memorable take away was from my Marine friend, David Penland, who often said to me, "we not only need to do what is right, we need to look like we are doing what is right."

We thank God for the privilege of leading this great church from 2002-2008, and the process of learning how to restore health to His bride. This all would be part of a blueprint we would use to help restore other broken churches, as well as churches that needed more than health restoration.

They would need nothing short of resurrection.

Cities Number Two & Three: SUBURBAN PHILADELPHIA

In January 2008, we received a phone call from the head deacon at First Baptist Church in Aston, Pennsylvania, asking us to consider a call to be their lead pastor. I had grown up in this church, and as an adult I served as associate pastor and student pastor for seven years. We met with the leaders at University and shared with them our burden and calling to Philadelphia, describing it as an extension of their ministry.

The move back to Aston would be personal. Many of the older adults in the church knew me as a teenager and young student pastor. We also had a very close relationship with the former pastor, which would actually serve to complicate the transition. We also brought six years of lead pastor and transition experience with us, as well as a deep love for the church and community, all of which would help us hit the ground running. First Baptist Church (FBC) had been in existence for more than 50 years. For the last 27 years, the church had but one pastor, who in my opinion had many fruitful years of ministry. The church had also sent many out into ministry, supported missionaries all over the world, helped plant churches, and sent dozens of trained staff couples all over the world. We received our own ministry call as a part of this church, learned a strong work ethic, and also a strong love for the very idea of the local church. We were also blessed to have had the experience of working for the previous pastor.

It was a great year to move back to Philadelphia. I have been an avid sports fan as long as I can remember. My dad took us to see every major sport at a young age and we grew up extremely loyal to Philadelphia sports franchises. We arrived in Philly to pastor

FBC in April 2008, the beginning of the Phillies baseball season. Watching baseball on TV and attending many games became a wonderful and much needed distraction during one of the hardest years of my life in full time ministry. When we pulled onto the property of FBC to candidate, my heart broke and I had a glimpse of what was before us. The property had visibly suffered, the spirit of the body was broken, and the church was on the verge of bankruptcy.

I preached in the morning and was introduced as a candidate, and that night 124 people voted yes. Significantly, six people who were members of the former pastor's family voted no. I do not think it was a vote against me per se, but rather was support for the out-going pastor retiring, as well as one against the church's deacons.

The financial position of the church was reflective of the spiritual state of the church—both on the edge of insolvency. Sunday attendance was averaging about 150, and the church operated a Christian school of 80 students and a daycare of 60 children. The church was $6.2 million dollars in debt. There were two bank mortgages totaling $3.2 million and an in-house loan (from members of church and community) of $2 million, with another $1 million in accounts payable, of which many were already in the hands of bill collectors.

There were many factors for this dire financial situation. The church had long been spending more money than it was making. There was a huge schism between the retiring pastor and the current deacon board. They were divided over the financial decisions, employee issues connected to his family, and the overall state of the church. The human tendency is to find someone to blame when things get bad, and there was plenty of blame to go around. Clearly, drastic decisions had to be made in a very short period of time, or decisions would be made for the church by banks and others.

All of this during the Great Recession of 2008. Property values plummeted and the country was in the middle of a banking crisis, all of which made the financial position of the church even more grave. Before the banking crisis, the projected value of the property at the time for the mortgage renewal was $6 million. Sadly, by 2008 the value of the property dropped to $4 million, and in 2009 it fell to $3 million. It was a morbid financial situation.

There was also an emotional sickness in the church. The leadership was divided, the former pastor and his family had been hurt, some of it was self-inflicted and some unfairly given.

The church was not only upside down financially, but also upside down in its ministry priorities because the church and school were so separated culturally, and the demographic of the school did not reflect the demographic of the church. Few in the church sent their children to the school—and no one in leadership did. It was really a house divided against itself. There was no love lost between the church and the school. The other emotional sickness flowed from the fact that the church had developed a bad reputation financially and had been on a five-year slide downward.

The church was also dying spiritually and was nearly on life-support. It was easy to blame the finances because they were quantifiable, but the divide between leadership and congregation was obvious. This was borne out in conversations with so many members during our first weeks back in town.

It was clearly a case where desperate times called for desperate measures.

I met with the leaders, and we put a short-term plan together to buy us a year to make more long-term permanent decisions. We met with five different banks and asked them if they would lend us $250,000 to help us bridge our finances for three to six months. On the Monday of our third week at the church, there was a very large sticker posted on the front door of the building. It had been placed there by the electric company, threatening to turn off the power if we did not pay more than $30,000 in 72 hours. This represented six months of unpaid electric bills.

Desperate times.

A lawyer joined a board member and I to meet with a local bank with whom we had a relationship—and they were sympathetic, lending us a quarter of a million dollars on a handshake. We knew the Lord had directed our words and the hearts of these men. We had been skeptical and weary going into the meeting. I later called the executive VP of the bank and asked him if he would trust me enough to extend our loan request to $500,000, instead of $250,000, enough to buy us a full year of breathing room. He laughed but agreed. He said he could not wait to see how this was going to work out for us.

We were now able to work on our long-term plan, and we knew what we needed to do. We prayed and talked to the church, and they voted unanimously to sell our building. We were asking $4 million which would cover only 60% of our debt, but it would pay off all of our secured debt. Six months later we received an offer of $3.2 million, enough to pay three of the mortgages, and four tax levies from the IRS—those levies from five years of unpaid payroll taxes. It was a measure of relief, but we were still physically and emotionally on life support.

And a spiritual dagger was coming.

We closed on the property in December 2009. The transaction was to take place at an Abstract and Title Office in the county seat. The day before settlement, we were served papers from the sheriff's office. They were from our former pastor threatening to block the sale of the property. The suit claimed the church owed his family and 50 others money from "in-house" loan agreements. The claim was for $160,000. We settled for ten cents on the dollar, which drained every last penny we had in our accounts following the sale of the property.

Looking back, that was the time of death for First Baptist Church. I stood before our church that Sunday and read the lawsuit. I told them the former pastor was not our enemy, and we loved him and his family. Our real enemy was Satan, and he was trying to destroy our church. We moved from the building that had been our home for 14 years and began meeting in a middle school auditorium. The kid's classes and nursery would meet in hallways separated by curtains.

Our church was now homeless.

One of the hardest parts of publicly sharing the lawsuit was presenting it to a room where 30-40 others were also owed substantial amounts of money. But this death of a church was necessary. It was painful, and emotional, but necessary for a healthy body to grow from its ashes.

We started a new church in December 2009—LIFE Church. Over the first 19 months we grew from 150 to 280 strong. We actually felt that the future for our church was strong, but we needed to put the past behind us. We had officially closed the First Baptist Church. We prayed for former leaders and members who were no longer part of our church, and we prayed for forgiveness for our past mistakes as a church. That was the culture in which LIFE Church was born.

Our church building had been purchased by another church from a different denomination. They met on three separate campuses. They had showed up at the closing with cameras, family members, and multiple representation. I was there just with our lawyer. Also there in the room were three bank representatives and an IRS representative waiting for their checks. We handed over the keys and walked out empty-handed. On the spot, I promised the Lord—and my lawyer—that we would never go through anything like that again.

Though we had started a vital new church, we were reminded of our past often. We still owed $1.7 million to several people who had put their trust in the now dead First

Baptist Church. We were a mobile church with very little overhead. We put a plan together to pay back our creditors in this order: widows, senior citizens, non-church members, church members, and then church officers. We sent a letter of intent to all 51 creditors and began making weekly payments. Because my salary was small, my wife got a part-time job, friends regularly invited me to speak in their churches, and I was able to speak at some youth camps. God provided. Word got out in the community that the former pastor had sued us, and in the next two years we were sued another fifteen times.

During that first year, we settled every debt out of court for ten cents on a dollar, bringing the outstanding debt down to $700,000. I was then sued by the former pastor's secretary, who falsely accused me of misconduct. The judge threw the case out—with prejudice—but an appeals judge advised the lawyers to settle out of court, anyway. We did that because she finally agreed that the allegations were false and was willing to sign a document to that effect. We settled her $250,000 claim for just $8,000. Lawsuit number 18 would prove to be the most difficult and became a game-changer for our church. The Securities and Exchange Commission, through the US District Attorney's office, sued us for mishandling church funds. The charges were directed at the former First Baptist Church, but because I was the pastor for 19 months before we closed it, I was named on the suit. My lawyer and I went to the S.E.C. office in Center City Philadelphia where I was deposed under oath, being recorded on tape with a court stenographer for four hours. It was brutal.

Our new church was in jeopardy of losing our 501(c3) status as a non-profit corporation. And if I were to be found guilty of mishandling funds, I could face a fine and maybe even jail time. Serious stuff. I knew in my heart the suit was directed more at the church's past, but it was still very scary. They collected all of our records and bank statements for the previous ten years (again, only 19 months of which were under my tenure). Four months later we were called in to discuss their findings. We sat down— tape recorder and stenographer present again—and the lawyer from the SEC told us that during the 19 months I lead the church, through the sale of the property and partial repayment of debts, everything had been done legally and ethically and in compliance with SEC regulations. She then told us that the US Attorney's, office along with the SEC, was going to file a claim against the former pastor. Then they discharged our debt.

At that time, LIFE Church had no permanent home. We were renting 1500 square feet of office space, but we were debt-free. It was surreal. We told the church family that the greatest financial work was complete and could start saving money for a new home.

God would let the comfortable become uncomfortable again. We were in talks with a commercial property owner, negotiating a lease for our church, when the high school we were leasing did not renew our lease because they were preparing for major renovation. For the second time, we moved our church into our tiny office space. We received a certificate of occupancy allowing us to have 120 people at a time, so we went from one service to four per weekend—one Saturday evening and three on Sunday morning. That Easter weekend, we added a fifth service and saw more than 750 in attendance. The office space was a great venue for us to recover from the season of litigation and strengthen our base as the Lord worked through our faithful people to build a strong bride for His glory.

The day after Easter, we contacted Marcus Hook Baptist Church (MHBC) in the neighboring township to see if we could lease extra space they had until we signed a lease and completed a build out. MHBC was an American Baptist Church started in 1789— that's right, 1789. They had 60,000 square feet of building space, but only 60 regular attenders. Their median membership age was 66. They had ten people in their nineties. When I contacted them, Mr. Jim Abbot, one of their deacons, told me that their pastor had just resigned. He told me, "we have a building and need a pastor, what do you think?"

Resurrection brings new life. Then healthy life multiplies!

We met with both church boards, then met together for a few church services. In June 2013, LIFE Church married Marcus Hook Baptist Church. We brought our memberships together, and MHBC was infused with 600 new family members. A "homeless" church family now had a home. The home we shared needed LIFE, and LIFE needed a home. It took a lot of work to bring the two families together. LIFE Church brought energy and excitement to Marcus Hook. Both churches were the answer to respective needs and had been brought together by Jehovah Jireh—our provider.

The transition process started all over again. Our "new" auditorium seated 500, so we went from five services in the office space to three in our new home. We wanted to honor the older members of MHBC, so we made our early service a senior-friendly traditional one. Something wonderful happened as a result—many of the older members of the LIFE Church started attending that service. It was both organic and authentic.

From the MHBC perspective, they saw "their" service double from 60 to more than 120. We would do baptisms between the two services, so everyone could be part of this special ministry expression. Our first baptism in the new church saw more people immersed (18) than MHBC had baptized the previous three years combined. Our combined churches worked toward unifying under one name, new by-laws and one shared vision.

Wonderful things occurred almost daily in this new church. The seniors that had held MHBC together for the past last 15 years said they prayed for the day they would see their building filled, and they were able to see it happen. Our LIFE Church members came alongside our new family and encouraged the members of MHBC. Our people were becoming one. Death had given way to new life. One elder from MHBC would tell me every Friday when we met for prayer that God was doing something special right in front of us.

And we needed to be careful not to get in the way.

We started over with a new plan for this new church. I had a friend in Texas who had two board members with experience putting together church by-laws. I flew to Dallas and went to a one-day conference about writing 501(c3). The two board members helped me develop an outline for the by-laws for our new ministry—one that we re-named The Bridge Church. The Bridge was about connecting past to present, the old church to the new church, and the church to the community.

The story of our seven-year journey is a testament to God's faithfulness. The physical, emotional, and spiritual rebirth of one church morphed into the rebirth of two. Resurrection brought forth life. Churches have wonderful people with honorable intentions to do great things for the kingdom. Having the opportunity to help lots of other pastors in their similar journey is an honor. We have helped pastors and leaders put their visions and plans together for their respective churches. I can honestly say that I have never talked to a pastor or church member who said, "we should set our sights lower and do less next year." We want to strive to do more for the sake of the gospel.

The problem with too many churches today is that they are not healthy enough to help other churches get healthy. Think about this: if a man 200-pounds overweight and smoking a cigarette tells you that he wants to help you get heathy, what would you say? Where would you go for training or coaching with your health needs? You would seek out a healthy doctor. Both First Baptist Church and Marcus Hook Baptist Church loved missionaries, wanted to see people saved, and wanted to make an impact on their community, but in order to do so, they needed to be healthy physically, emotionally, and spiritually.

The story of cities two and three is about two churches, with four different names, that became ONE—The Bridge Church, now being pastored by Aaron Harding. We are proud of Aaron and his sweet wife Martha, and the great work God is doing in and through them for their community. Aaron was called in 2015 when we accepted our next assignment in Dallas, Texas. The Bridge Church is a testimony of endurance, integrity, protection and God's faithfulness. They are a presence in Delaware County, Pennsylvania and still making Jesus famous today.

City Number FOUR: RICHARDSON, TEXAS

Since I used a sports anecdote at the beginning of the last section, I will do the same for this one. If someone would have told me I would be pastoring in Dallas, Texas while I was in Bible College, or living in Philadelphia, I would have laughed at them. Dallas is the belly of the beast for Philadelphia Eagles fans. We loved to visit, but while there we would be in Eagle gear from head to toe. But sometimes a calling of God is not about a city or region, like missionaries or a church planter would speak about. This assignment was about a local body, Canyon Creek Baptist Church in Richardson Texas.

Canyon Creek Baptist Church (CCBC) was planted in Richardson Texas in the early 1970s. The church began about the same time as the great Prestonwood Baptist Church, and for a few years the two congregations had paralleled journeys. The former pastor has been a lifelong friend of mine. He was the pastor I consulted about the process of putting together by-laws for our church in Philadelphia, he recommended me to two of Canyon Creek's board members who had experience with local church legal structure. I had flown to Dallas for two days in the spring of 2014 and received a great deal of help putting our new by-laws together. While working with the Canyon Creek board members back then, they asked a lot of questions about our journey while contemplating their own difficult situation. In retrospect, the Lord was clearly connecting us for the future.

In 2012, the board of CCBC had asked the man who was then the pastor to resign because they wanted to take the church in a different direction. I am not going to share any personal opinions about the story preceding our call, just the facts and timeline. When they asked that former pastor to resign, they presented my friend to the church as their candidate for the pastorate, but the congregational vote fell short. The church then called for a second vote on the same man because the first vote had been very close, and there was division in the church. But again, the candidate didn't receive enough votes. The board then asked some members who were causing division in the church to leave. This was followed by a third vote. This time my friend was called as the new pastor of Canyon Creek. But less than two years later, he was forced to resign due to a personal moral failure.

CCBC contacted me a few months after my friend's resignation, asking me to advise them about what to do next. I walked them through a process of searching for and calling the right candidate. But all the while, as I listened to them talk about the state of their church, God was burdening my heart for them. When my friend resigned, he was the third of the last four pastors who was forced to resign because of moral failure.

The church operated a Christian School whose past leadership also had moral failures. And the church was in serious financial trouble. With Sunday attendance running close to 200, the Christian school had 140 students enrolled, and there were 60 children in the ministry's daycare center. The church owed $6 million on their 180,000 square foot facility. Needless to say, Canyon Creek Baptist Church was on life-support. When I advised them about a plan, a process, and personality of man to call, they asked me to pray about coming.

I knew in my heart that the Lord was moving us.

Candidating was a whirlwind process over a weekend. I met with the board, some key families, and then there was a "town hall" meeting on Saturday night. I preached on Sunday morning and the congregation voted Sunday night. The town hall meeting was a portend for us—a peek into our future. Some of the questioners grandstanded a bit— giving lengthy statements about the board, the former pastors, directional preferences, financial perceptions. The meeting went quite long, and it was a very sad display of a broken body. One woman told me how she was against nepotism and asked if I intended to hire my family members. She said she thought I should not be allowed to do so. I told her, "do not vote for me, because I will not be limited on the people I would hire."

The process would be that the board approved positions and salaries, and I hired the people.

Needless to say, this lady was an antagonist from day one.

One man pontificated about the horrible position the church was in financially and asked if I would stay in the event the church had to sell the property, close the school, and move. As I've said, I answered his question with a question, asking him if he would stay if everything happened as he predicted. The church was very divided over methodology, and both sides were steadfastly against each other. About a third of the church wanted to go back to "the old ways," because the pastor who had just resigned had moved "too fast." I really couldn't blame them for feeling that way because his credibility was nil to them. The rest of the folks seemed to want to be young-family oriented and outward reaching—but even they were divided among themselves. We knew the task was going to be just as difficult as the major operation in Philadelphia. Following great services that Sunday, morning and evening, the church voted to call us, 178 to 1.

We arrived in Richardson in April 2015. Our early plan was to see what vital signs of life existed in the church. There was enough cash on hand in the church accounts to sustain us for maybe a year and a half—the proceeds from loans made to the church by some of the members. We needed to diagnose whether the church was merely sick, or actually dead. There were a few signs of life. There were some wonderful, committed people who truly loved the Lord and the church.

But there were also some very antagonistic members. I believe the antagonism, though somewhat understandable, was not at all justified. When a new pastor is called to a dying church, it does not take long for cynical church members to associate the new leader with the sins of the past.

Our honeymoon did not last long.

Phase one of our plan was to release employees who no longer wanted to work at the church or the school. We wanted to make sure the ministry staff was fully behind the leadership team. Some church members were sad to see some staffers leave, but overall, this initiative was supported.

During phase two, we presented three things to the church board, things that needed to change. We had a terrible reputation in the community. We had the church vote to update our name, cancel Sunday evening services (only a dozen or so showed up, typically), and stop having monthly business meetings in favor of quarterly ones. The first two initiatives were quickly passed unanimously. We changed our name to Canyon Creek Church—not in an "anti-Baptist" move, but simply to change public perception.

We cancelled Sunday night services with the understanding that we would be starting small groups in homes. This also passed with a 100% affirmative vote. I thought we were home free because monthly business meetings were redundant and very little could be reported in such a short period of time. But this is when the health of the church was truly revealed. The last and, from my perception, least controversial initiative turned out to be the beginning of a two-year war with a group in our church. I was accused of hiding things, not being transparent, and protecting the deacons from mistakes they were making. You would have thought I had committed a big, disqualifying sin. After several hours of deliberation, I asked the church to vote on it, the motion was seconded, the motion received 80% of the vote. After the vote, during that same meeting, we presented the initiative as adopted, and the woman who became my main antagonist told me in front of the church, that my tenure would be short if I was planning on leading behind closed doors. The church was on life support, and it was clear that we needed to make some drastic decisions and changes.

Antagonists are an interesting dynamic in an unhealthy church. They usually reveal more about the complainer than the complaint itself. There was one observation I remember from our early days at CCBC. I would ask in public meetings, "Do you think our church needs to make some serious changes?" This question never hit a resistant answer. I also asked, "What changes do you think we need to make?" One answer in particular was funny because it came from an antagonist, "That's what we are paying you to do!" My response was "Then let me do my job."

There is a book called, Antagonists in the Church, by Kenneth Haugk. It is a great resource for pastors dealing with difficult congregants. Haugk guides us through a process of identifying and dealing with destructive and antagonistic behavior. The book was given to me by a mentor.

We discovered another serious problem. The leadership did not tell the church why the pastor who committed immorality had to resign. This helped to fuel the antagonistic flame, because they were right in the sense that there had not been full disclosure in some areas of our ministry.

The church was in financial trouble, with too much debt and too many monthly obligations. We prepared to make major financial shifts to help the church, but the finances had not been tampered with during my tenure, nor that of my immediate predecessor. We had a great, loyal, and extremely honest CFO, as well as a Forensic Accountant who kept very clean records. Money gets so much attention because it needs to. It seems that bad money problems are often indicative of deeper issues in a church. This was certainly the case for Canyon Creek. We talked about money, enrollment, giving, tuition, and pointed blaming fingers everywhere. The problem was in our past and in our leadership.

In the summer of 2016, our board met with a consultant to discuss the future of our ministry. We arrived at a unanimous conclusion that we had too much building space and too much debt. Accordingly, we needed to sell the building and close the school. We could then move our church to a smaller, more efficient facility, and then truly focus on the actual mission of the church. The church was $7 million in debt, and the school was running a deficit of $560,000 annually. We had our property appraised at $10.5 million. We voted on it as a church and communicated this to our school, with plenty of notice. We received a very good offer from the Seventh Day Adventists of Dallas for $10 million, and we negotiated to rent from them for a year at $5000 per month for our church.

The closing of our school was understandably difficult and painful during the second half of that school year. School families were hurt and some lashed out at the church, but the church could not afford to lose half of a million dollars per year any longer. This was hard because many good people would need to find jobs, sophomores and juniors would not be able to graduate from a school they had attended for many years, and it was the end of an era for a school that existed for 40 years. So, yes, it was somewhat emotional. At the same time, this was not all that hard because the school families and school staff actually wanted nothing to do with Canyon Creek Baptist Church. There was a great divide between church and school. When I arrived the previous year, I interviewed every teacher on staff to build relationships and a bridge to the church. Ninety-five of the school staff members did not attend our church. More than 60% of the school staff viewed our church unfavorably. This was because of the generational sin that prevailed in the church—immorality.

The church had even been the subject of a national news report in the early 1980s, because one of the former pastors was having sexual relationships with multiple women on the staff. His trouble started when he was arrested for shoplifting condoms from a local store, which made the local news. Shortly after, he was caught having multiple affairs, as was one of the school administrators. The school lost confidence in the church's leadership and the divide grew.

My "school" reputation preceded me. The families of the school knew that I came from a ministry in Philadelphia where we had made the decision to close a school because it was losing money annually, and they saw the writing on the wall. But we did not come to Dallas with the intention of closing the school or selling the property, we came to do what the Lord lead us to do to bring the church to a place of physical, emotional, and spiritual health. Even though it was difficult, and it took some extra support from our board and church, closing the school and selling our property were the right decisions.

This was a big step in healing the church physically, but set us back a bit emotionally, and we did not begin to touch the hem of the garment spiritually. The building was sold in January 2017. We had a comprehensive plan for closing the school, one that included help for 100% of our staff to transition to new jobs successfully. We hired a business executive whose responsibility it was to help the school finish its final six months strong. We hired a company to handle the transcripts, and helped our juniors graduate with a Canyon Creek Christian Academy diploma with help from Collin County Community

College. The school officially closed May 31, 2017. When we sold the building earlier that year, we paid our mortgages and debt totaling $7.5 million. We started making plans to close the church and start a new one.

I was approached by a representative of the board and encouraged to close the church down, as well, at the end of that June. I was offered an attractive severance package and was told that we had actually finished what we started two years earlier. I went home and prayed about this but did not believe the Lord wanted us to leave. We tenderly rejected the gracious offer and made plans to replant the church.

Canyon Creek Church's board voted to give half of the remaining proceeds to the new church and the other half to missionaries and church planters all over the world.

We met with 25 leaders from the church and put a plan together to launch Warehouse Church. Canyon Creek voted to close the former church on June 30, 2017. The official start date of Warehouse Church was July 1, 2017. We were very blessed to meet in the old gym of the building we just sold to the Seventh Day Adventists for our first 13 months. This was humbling because for a little over a year, every Sunday and Wednesday we entered a building we sold and that represented so many difficult decisions during our first two years in Dallas. We experienced quite a bit of fallout from the school and church closures, and in the first month of Warehouse Church the average weekly attendance was just 94 people, quite a fall from the glory days when the church ran 1,200. It was humbling for me personally, as we had grown back to around 500 during my short tenure, only to see it slide away. I started wondering if the board was right and that maybe we should have shut the church down and moved on to our next church project. But we did not have peace about moving on and felt strongly that we were not finished in Richardson. There was something still missing—part of the story remained to be written.

The Warehouse Church spent its first six months in recovery. We had to recover personally, as did our staff, the board that came with us, and the entire church family. We had a large exodus of members and leaders when we closed the former church and school. This included people who were present the very first day Canyon Creek was planted in the 1970s—they stayed until the closing service on June 24, 2017.

That church had a starting date and an ending date.

Many of those who left were not really angry or bitter—just sad and broken. The church as a whole knew this was the right decision, but the reality of it was harder than expected. We lost over half of the church. Only two of the nine board members joined the new church, so while we knew the Lord wanted us to start Warehouse Church, we were still missing something.

By the next January, we knew we needed to move to a new facility, one that represented a final and total separation from our past. We looked at more than 40 potential venues, approached a few dozen churches about potential partnerships, and then one day found exactly what the Lord had prepared for us.

The Warehouse Church found its "Warehouse."

We found a building to lease, negotiated a fantastic price, prepaid the rent for two years so we could grow into our payment, and then put a strategy together to raise the funds we needed to complete our envisioned build out. We needed to raise $500,000 for that part of the project. I called an old friend to help us put a capital fund-raising campaign together, but God did not bring him to us to help us merely raise money— Pastor Mike Schirle was sent from God to help us raise the dead.

Earlier, when I was describing the story of our Philadelphia church, the words flowed easily from my memory. It was a joy to remember and record. That story was very clear, historically. It is easy to see where God directed, guided, and provided. We can look back at landmarks that were left behind and significant decisions that the Lord lead us to make to see now how God is Sovereign, Provider, and Sustainer of His Church. However, when you are in the middle of things, the story is not always so clear. We were able to draw from so much of our financial experiences from both of our previous ministries, legal experience from the lawsuits, and real estate experience from moving. But we had one last piece to make this transition complete.

We needed a funeral.

Pastor Mike Schirle came to work with our leaders to put a stewardship plan together. We had a great plan and the leaders bought in. It was a good season for us, and six months after we began, we were finally able to separate ourselves from the whirlwind of transactions and the sadness of closures. Now, we could focus on reaching new people. The church doubled in the next six months, and we were averaging just north of 200 by January 2018. When Mike came, we sat down after a few days of meeting with key leaders and he asked me, "What happened here? Give me the whole story." He also knew the former pastor very well. We told him of the moral failure in this man's life, that it was not just a one-time incident but a lifetime issue. We shared how our church took an aggressive stand with him, sending him to a long-term care facility for counseling and recovery, how we helped his family move and tried to be a part of his restoration. He asked me if we had ever, as a church, confessed the sins of our past. He asked if the evil of sexual sin from our church's past had been prayed over and washed by the blood of the lamb.

What he was really asking me was if we ever called the TIME OF DEATH for Canyon Creek Church, putting everything bad behind us so we could truly start anew. This was the missing piece of the puzzle—necessary for the health of our church.

We were still in the old gym, five months away from moving. We planned a Good Friday service to prepare us for Easter and the future of Warehouse Church. The team set up a few hundred folding chairs in the largest space that was clean enough to meet in at the new property. We made two banners quoting 2 Corinthians 5:17. The first one read, "Old Things Passed Away", and the second said, "All Things New." We had dry erase boards and markers under both banners, and while we sang a couple songs, we asked the people to write with the permanent marker on the new wall—to write great memories and positive things we wanted the Lord to bring with us from the former church to the future ministry of Warehouse Church. There were great things written about conversions, marriages restored, babies dedicated, baptisms, missionaries supported, churches planted, and so much more. It was moving as members old and young were so ready to share great stories. I then told the church: "We are taking the good and leaving the bad behind." I talked to them about the past of Canyon Creek, the moral issues, the spiritual decay that followed, the complacency, the gossip, and the negative spirit that lived in that building. I confessed to them that I had been through more spiritual oppression during the previous two years than I had experienced during my whole life. I told them that the temptations for failure in my own life were very real and the attack was strong. I wrote five major sins of our past.

We prayed for forgiveness for each. We prayed for the spirit of adultery to leave our church and the former facility as well. We prayed for guidance, protection, and for the Lord to forgive our church of the mistakes of our past. We had one of the charter members come up to the board and erase every sin I listed. Then we took communion and rejoiced. The time of death was Good Friday and the resurrection of our church happened as we celebrated the Resurrected Savior on Easter Morning.

We had visitors and 300 in attendance that day, but the joy was overshadowed by the significance of what we had done on Friday. We declared and acknowledged the life, death, and resurrection of our church. We encouraged our body as we remembered Canyon Creek, not to talk about the sin or other perceived issues, but to remember the great influence and impact it had. We thanked God for our "sending church!"

We were starting fresh and new.

I believe when Canyon Creek was started in the early 1970s the Lord knew the day it would die, as well. The death is no longer sad for me, because it ushered in new life. The physical and emotional sickness in the church was certainly a major problem, but not as much as the fact that the church spiritually was dead. To try to put this on one man, or one decision is impossible and wrong. We need to remember who our true enemy is; it is not the board member who went rogue, or the pastor who failed morally, but the author of destruction and father of lies, Satan. He is the one who hated the church and strategically took out key leaders one by one. He attacked the school, the church families, and the church itself, for in its death, Satan knows the influence of the gospel can be strangled.

When resurrection takes place in a body, NEW LIFE begins. This is a great testimony to the faithfulness of so many wonderful people that we get to do life with, but it was not us, and it's not our church. It belongs to the one who started it, paid for it and sustains it, the Lord Jesus Christ.

We moved into our facility in August. Our build out was completed that December. We hit 400 in attendance for the first time in October—and 500 for the first time in December. We are still raising money to finish our build out and working hard to reach and impact our community. We are praying that the Lord provides for us to buy the whole building someday. We currently lease about 40% of it. We would like to use part of our building for a mission organization that we are involved with called MANNA Worldwide, and even have an office for a church consulting ministry we would like to start to help churches revitalize or resurrect from the dead.

The tale of four cities is that the Lord has a plan for Warehouse Church and for your church. The focus of this chapter was not about the failures of a few, but of the faithfulness of THE ONE, our Lord Jesus Christ. He has a plan for His church, His bride, to be His voice and His presence here on earth until He comes back someday to take us home. His plan for the church is flawless: be witnesses in Jerusalem, Judea, Samaria and to the ends of the earth. As witnesses, he wants us to say what Peter and John said in Acts 4:20, "We cannot stop talking about the things we have seen and heard."

The four cities story precedes the next section of more great stories of struggles, bad decisions, great leaders, and the Great Physician's plan to heal sick churches or even resurrect dead ones. A friend recently asked me, "can you tell me how to do this, how to resurrect our dead church?"

I think when we realize that the "removal of sickness" really symbolizes the removal of self or flesh, this is the starting point. Churches are not like human beings until they start becoming less like Jesus and more like everyday people. We will discuss strategies to help get churches to a place of health or new life. I believe with all of my heart that this can happen when we do what my friend John Bullock said to me in Philadelphia: "Pastor, we need to pray that God would not let us get in the way of something wonderful He is doing here!"

Sin is real. Church struggles may be very unique but remember these two things: the struggles are with SIN, and we are not the first church that had a letter written to us about cleaning up a mess. The church at Corinth had two letters written to them by Paul to clean up their body, and the church in Galatia had a pretty stern letter written to them about healing their body, as well. Christian schools, church programs, and other ministry initiatives are not bad things. Money and property are not bad things, and even debt is not always a bad thing. The physical challenges we worked through in our churches that led to emotional hurt, then spiritual challenges, and then breakthroughs, started because the human heart is extraordinarily wicked (See Jeremiah 17:9). When we get in the way, God has this amazing gift of forgiveness and forgetfulness. He forgives us and removes our sins when we seek His forgiveness.

Our prayer for Warehouse Church, as it is for your church, is that we would pursue physical, emotional, and spiritual health and BECOME THE CHURCH that He has called and equipped us to be.

Chapter 4

You can do it if you try, V-I-C-T-O-R-Y

In the previous four chapters I use the words "us" and "we" when I talk about "our" calling and "our" ministry. The us, we, and our is my family. I had the privilege of marrying my high school sweetheart, Kimberly Voegele. We had our 36th anniversary on May 18, 2021. She is the only girl I ever said "I love you" to, she's as pretty to me today after decades of marriage as she was the day I took her out on our first date when we were 16 years old. We were super young when we got married 2 months before our 19th birthdays. We have been in ministry life together since we surrendered when we were 24 years old with 2 children. Every paper I wrote at Baptist Bible College, she typed for me. Every ministry assignment we gave our lives to, we did together. She is faithful, loyal, has an incredible work ethic, was the best mom our children could have asked for, and is an even better grandmother (or, as she would prefer to be called, "Kiki") to our five beautiful grandkids! She was custom-made for me—I really believe this! Each church we lead, and the victories I wrote about followed many days, months, and years of personal and professional heartache. If anyone ever deserved an award for just participating, it would be she.

We understand "participation awards" because we were in the front row when our daughters would receive them at all day cheerleading events. Kim and I have 4 great daughters, who served with us in every ministry we have been a part of. Kristina, Katie, Kelsea, and Emily were all very active in their schools, participating in athletics and music, and three of them were also cheerleaders. With all of the challenges that come with raising four girls — teenage years, puberty, being the only man in my house, hugs from one and crying from another daily, the hardest thing that I have ever done is sit through a full 10-hour day of a cheerleading competition. There are two reasons this is painful, it's ten hours of face-hurt smiling and loud noises, and both no one and everyone wins. Cheerleading is the "sport" that had to be the first to introduce the idea of a participation trophy. We sat through a day-long marathon of competition, and during the awards ceremony there were 44 awards given—to a total of 44 teams. No one went home empty-handed.

In this cheerleading competition culture, everyone was a winner. Ministry is funny because even though we do not like to admit it, ministries are kind of in competition with one another. We say what Paul said when we get a burst of spirituality in our lives, "I press towards the mark of the high calling of God through Christ Jesus." We want to fight the good fight, finish the course and keep the faith, but we kind of compete too. Pastors (myself included) love talking about our high days, we are infamous for telling guest speakers at our churches, "I think we were a little down today." We love posting the big baptism day videos and telling all of our pastor buddies about our big day stats. Sometimes we know our competition is not each other, and we are all fighting for souls, but sometimes we also want to be the biggest and best. Missionaries do this as well (I was one of these also). It seems the most passionate testimonies share the most extreme statistics such as the most populated window on the whole earth, the hottest climate, the coldest climate and the farthest distance. I promise you that I have even heard someone say, "We do ministry in a public school which is the largest high school in the universe."

I think a participation trophy in ministry should be enough. I don't mean settling or being complacent, but simply staying in it means something and deserves at least an "atta-boy!" I went to a national meeting of our tribe and saw a pastor there who I attended school with though we were never friends. I did not dislike him, but we ran in different groups. However, when I observed him for a while I thought, "What a great guy!" He's still with the girl he married in college, they are a great ministry team, they have great adult kids, way to go! I actually went up to him and told him I was cheering for him in the last row of the stands. We were not close, but I admired his family and faithfulness. I don't think he needed my approval at all, but that guy deserves a participation trophy!

I have asked a group of young men and women that I grew up in ministry with to tell their stories of revitalization or resurrection at the church or a former church they led. We did not all go to the same school or at the same time, but we are connected through the Baptist Bible Fellowship in one way or another. There are similarities and distinctions to every story, and the end of the story for each of these churches has not yet been written! I sent a short questionnaire to each of them, representing churches all over the United States. There are 7 lead pastors and 1 female associate pastor. I sent each pastor a letter (as follows) with 7 questions.

Thanks for your help my brothers!

The premise of my dissertation is that churches (the living bride of Christ), like our bodies, (which were made in God's likeness) have a body, soul, and spirit. I believe there are dying churches that need revitalization, and dead churches that need to be resurrected. Churches die physically, emotionally and spiritually—they can be revitalized or resurrected in the same three areas.

Physical sickness or death in a church can be a result of:

The facilities being neglected over years

The finances being in disarray or not living within the means of the budget

The methods of the church being irrelevant to the needs of the community

Recent or long-term mass migration

The church has not shown growth in a long time

Emotional sickness or death occurs in Churches that are:

Stuck because of things they love that have nothing to do with reaching people (such as staff members who have been there for 25 years and are bitter and useless)

Styles of worship that are irrelevant and poorly executed

"We've always done it that way" is a core value

No leadership, plan, or follow through

Spiritually immature members

Leadership being disjointed

No vision or purpose.

Spiritual death or sickness can result from:

Sexual or generational pervasive sin

Major financial failure from stealing or mismanagement

A major church split

Any kind of major occurrence that would lead to the need to shut down the current church and relaunching.

With some of this in mind: Can you answer for me the following questions:

1. *Names(s) of your church—old and current:*

2. *How long have you been there?*

3.   *Would you say your church was dying—needing revitalization, or dead—needing resurrecting?*

4.   *Without naming names, would you be able to describe major things that happened that led to your church's death or near-death experience?*

5.   *Can you describe a process that led to your church's breakthrough?*

6.   *What are some health indicators you can measure in your church (vital signs of life)?*

7.   *How can you make sure that when it is time to move on (retire, call time of death) that you will be leaving your church healthy for the next generation?*

Here are their responses:

Pastor Anthony Milas, Lead Pastor of **Granite United Church**, Salem, New Hampshire

1.   Name(s) of your church—old and current:

   a.   Old: Granite State Baptist Church

   b.   New: Granite United Church

2.   How long have you been there? Since 1998

3.   Would you say your church was dying—needing revitalization, or dead—needing resurrecting?

   a.   Granite State was dead, so 6 months into it on a Wednesday night, I preached a funeral message and we buried it.

   b.   The following Sunday we relaunched Granite United with 40/50 adults.

4.   Without naming names, would you be able to describe major things that happened that led to your church's death or near-death experience?

   a.   Lack of getting new people through the doors and then reaching new people.

   b.   Existing people used same language but different dictionaries.

5.   Can you describe a process that led to your church's breakthrough?

   a.   Buried what was dead.

   b.   Began painting a picture of what could be.

    c.   Began the process of turning our reputation around in the surrounding community.

    d.   Began building teams for where we were going not where we were.

    e.   Made evangelism the CENTER OF ALL PREACHING.

6.   What are some health indicators you can measure in your church (vital signs of life)?

    a.   Salvations.

    b.   Bibles handed out at the alter (public response).

    c.   Baptisms in relation to Bibles handed out.

    d.   Dream Team growth (volunteers).

    e.   If we are reproducing service, a campus, or church plant.

    f.   Growth in giving.

    g.   And people in community.

7.   How can you make sure that when it is time to move on (retire, call time of death) that you will be leaving your church healthy for next generation?

    a.   I don't believe our church is built on my personality.

    b.   I have established strong voices who lead in the vision.

We have a shared team ministry concept (next man up).

Granite will not need to look outside her walls for next lead pastor.

Granite United Church has 7 campuses with 11 weekend services. They have 2500 people that currently attend their church, and they have planted 6 autonomous churches.

Pastor Craig Killinen, BridgePoint Church, **Temperance, Michigan**

1.   Name(s) of your church—old and current:

    a.   Old: First Baptist Church

    b.   New: BridgePoint Church

2.   How long have you been there? Since 2006, Lead Pastor since 2011

3.   Would you say your church was dying—needing revitalization, or dead—needing resurrecting?

    a.   Dying needing Revitalization

4.   Without naming names, would you be able to describe major things that happened that led to your church's death or near-death experience?

    a.   We were stuck in our ways catering to the needs of the already found.

    b.   We had people on staff who were just here for a paycheck, that had zero relationships with others, and zero passion to do ministry.

    c.   Church people had become very comfortable going through the motions.

5.   Can you describe a process that led to your church's breakthrough?

    a.   Church fire dislodged us from our very comfortable mindset.

    b.   Future decision to rebuild on old property caused some existing leadership (elders) to resign and leave openings for new leadership (elders) who have bought-in to the mantra of helping people find and follow Jesus that our church has developed.

    c.   With certain staff members' "security blanket" now gone, it allowed us to make decisions involving staff that should have been made years ago.

6.   What are some health indicators you can measure in your church (vital signs of life)?

    a.   Small groups are growing.

    b.   New families each week.

    c.   Young families each week.

    d.   People in services each week that are currently sitting in chair 1 around the table (they need a relationship with Christ).

    e.   People are being open and honest about their struggles and battles and not pretending to be something they are not or pretending as if everything is fine, when it's not.

7.   How can you make sure that when it is time to move on (retire, call time of death) that you will be leaving your church healthy for next generation?

    a.   Developing and Training up leaders as we go.

    b.   Giving others more responsibility even if they don't do things quite like I would.

    c.   Making Jesus and Jesus ALONE famous. It's not about anybody else, including and especially ME, it's all about Jesus.

BridgePoint Church currently runs 350 people with 2 weekend services. They are meeting in a temporary facility until their rebuild is finished.

Pastor Dan Woodcock, Cornerstone Church, **Gadsden, Alabama**

1. Name(s) of your church—old and current:

    a. Old: The Gathering in Gadsden

    b. New: Cornerstone Church.

2. How long have you been there? Since 2015

3. Would you say your church was dying—needing revitalization, or dead—needing resurrecting?

    a. Our church was in desperate need of resurrecting! It was on its way to being dead!

4. Without naming names, would you be able to describe major things that happened that led to your church's death or near-death experience?

    a. The previous pastor of the church split the congregation and all that was left was about 65 people, average age 60! There was no moral failure or anything illegal.

    b. Basically, it came down to elder-led vs. pastor-led.

    c. The pastor, even though he said the church was elder led, followed only what he felt God told him to do regardless of the elders' input. It came down to his way or no way. If God spoke to him, that was the final word.

    d. He split the church on graduation Sunday 2014.

    e. Also, our church was in downtown Gadsden, but we didn't reach anyone in the downtown area.

5. Can you describe a process that led to your church's breakthrough?

    a. I was on staff as the next gen pastor, working toward a church plant we were planning in Denver.

    b. I told the church and remaining leadership that the only way I knew how to help them was to start over. I was a church planter and we could replant this church.

    c.   I told them that I wanted to reach people in our local area, and those who were unchurched, de-churched, and far from God. They all bought in.

6.   What are some health indicators you can measure in your church (vital signs of life)?

    a.   We have seen God's hand in so many incredible ways! We average about 300 on any given Sunday now. We have grown by over 25% this past year.

    b.   We saw 54 people place their faith in Christ this past year, baptizing 13 of them.

    c.   We had 256 first-time guests this past year.

    d.   We have over 100 people serving in some way to make Sunday's happen.

    e.   Our small group ministry continues to grow with each semester.

    f.   Our giving is slowly increasing, and people are growing from sporadic givers to extravagant givers.

    g.   People are excited, we continue to reach new people and the life of the church is hopping nowadays!

7.   How can you make sure that when it is time to move on (retire, call time of death) that you will be leaving your church healthy for next generation?

    a.   We're trying to develop a healthy leadership structure so that all of the responsibility doesn't fall on one guy's shoulders.

    b.   I'm working to create systems for our church so that everything doesn't have to go through me, but there's freedom for others to take initiative and lead.

Pastor Esteban Alvarez, Acceso Veritcal, **Montevideo, Uruguay**

1.   Name(s) of your church—old and current:
2.   We actually took two and made one

    a.   Old: Primera Iglesia Bautista Bíblica Fundamental de Carrasco (First Fundamental Bible Baptist Church in Carrasco)

    b.   Old: Iglesia Bautista Bíblica de las Tres Cruces (Bible Baptist Church of the Three Crosses)

    c.   New: Vertical Access (Baptist Church in the Books)

3. How long have you been there? Since 2017

4. Would you say your church was dying—needing revitalization, or dead—needing resurrecting?

    a. Dead needing resurrecting.

5. Without naming names, would you be able to describe major things that happened that led to your church's death or near-death experience?

    a. Leadership issues.

    b. A bit of legalism.

    c. Stuck in the "old ways."

    d. Not knowing how to read cultural changes.

6. Can you describe a process that led to your church's breakthrough?

    a. Sat on the bench for a year.

    b. Churches declined to no people.

    c. Open heart conversations with pastors.

    d. Pause (I asked them to take a 3 week break and go to other churches to observe things).

    e. Strategic planning for a soft launch.

    f. Vision for the new church.

    g. Magnify the Gospel instead of the changes.

    h. Celebrate the opportunity.

    i. Maximize the potential in leaders (old & new.)

    j. PLAN in every area.

    k. Prayer & staff meetings every week.

7. What are some health indicators you can measure in your church (vital signs of life)

    a. First time visitors staying at the church, experiencing salvation & Baptism.

    b. Numerical growth in attendance.

    c. Rejection from other local churches.

    d. Volunteers in every event, weekly & special events.

    e.   Offerings.

8. How can you make sure that when it is time to move on (retire, call time of death) that you will be leaving your church healthy for next generation?

    a.   Constant Training.

    b.   Casting the Vision periodically.

    c.   Equip young adults to future leadership.

Brian Moore, Crosspointe Church, Anaheim, California

1. Name(s) of your churches—old and current:

2. We had/have two sites

    a.   Old: Calvary Baptist Church

    b.   New: Crosspointe Church Anaheim

    c.   Old: Ventura Baptist Church

    d.   New: Crosspointe Church Ventura

3. How long have you been there? Since 2008

4. Would you say your church was dying—needing revitalization or dead—needing resurrecting?

    a.   Dead needing resurrecting on both sites.

5. Without naming names, would you be able to describe major things that happened that led to your church's death or near-death experience?

    a.   Bad leadership.

    b.   Moral Failure.

    c.   Sexual Sin.

    d.   Financial Sin.

    e.   A lack of addressing problems.

    f.   Three Churches in one in Ventura.

6. Can you describe a process that led to your church's breakthrough?

7. Ed, I've developed these 12 Blocks out of a study of the questions I asked on the revitalization page. I prioritized them and made them alliterative, just like I was taught in preaching workshop. [grin] The Revitalization Building Blocks:

    a.   Christ Builds the Church.

   b.   Calling to Revitalize.

   c.   Challenges Pinpointed.

   d.   Commitment to First Impressions.

   e.   Courage to Make Necessary Changes.

   f.   Core Group of Revitalizers.

   g.   Culture Shifts.

   h.   Confronting Controllers.

   i.   Casting Vision.

   j.   Community Outreach.

   k.   Creating Systems.

   l.   Celebrating Victories.

8.   What are some health indicators you can measure in your church (vital signs of life)?

   a.   Baptisms.

   b.   First and second time Guests tracked through guest cards.

   c.   Numerical growth in attendance.

   d.   People participating in growth groups.

   e.   Radical Mentoring Group attendance.

   f.   50% of attendance volunteering.

   g.   Offerings.

9.   How can you make sure that when it is time to move on (retire, call time of death) that you will be leaving your church healthy for next generation?

   a.   Leadership Pipeline. Making sure I'm not the bottleneck of leadership.

   b.   Allowing my staff and key leaders to lead even when it's different than the way I may do it.

   c.   Test the results (trust but verify).

   d.   I can have growth or control. I can't have both.

   e.   Setting up a healthy leadership structure with accountability and freedom to lead.

   f.   By-Laws and governing documents.

g. Financial Margin.

Crosspointe Church has two campuses that facilitate three weekend services and their weekend attendance is 1500.

Randy Harp, former pastor of Grand Oaks Church, **Humble TX**

1. Now Editor of Baptist Bible Tribune
2. Ed, I will answer these from the perspective of the church I pastored in Houston before moving to Springfield.
3. Name(s) of your church—old and current:
    a. Old: North Park Baptist Church (North Freeway Baptist Church 30 years before)
    b. New: Grand Oaks Church (named for the neighborhood closest to the church)
4. How long have you been there? I was there four years.
5. Would you say your church was dying—needing revitalization, or dead—needing resurrecting?
    a. It was dying and in need of revitalization.
6. Without naming names, would you be able to describe major things that happened that led to your church's death or near-death experience?
    a. Major financial moral failure from previous pastor (this is what got the attention of the church).
    b. Other, hidden factors that were not being addressed.
    c. Empowering poor leaders with too much authority.
    d. City planning decisions (When church relocated to the property, there was an understanding of where a major road would be located. due to the International Airport moving their runway locations, the major road was moved ½ mile, which eliminated the church from having frontage visibility).
    e. Lack of evangelistic zeal.
    f. Lack of church focusing on local community (demographics within the church did not match those of the community closest to the church).
7. Can you describe a process that led to your church's breakthrough?

    a.   Focus on restoring health.

    b.   Building trust in leadership.

    c.   Being accountable.

    d.   Evangelistic emphasis on the local community.

8. What are some health indicators you can measure in your church (vital signs of life)?

    a.   First time guests.

    b.   Second time guests.

    c.   Salvations.

    d.   Baptisms.

    e.   Small group involvement.

    f.   Ministry involvement.

    g.   Percentage giving.

9. How can you make sure that when it is time to move on (retire, call time of death) that you will be leaving your church healthy for next generation?

10. I have left and even though the church is smaller now than when I left, it is healthier.

- Choose to do one of two things …
  a.   Focus on reaching the community around them OR
  b.   Relocate to a new community that matched their demographics.

- Since I have left, the church sold their building/property and has purchased new property and will begin building soon. The vision was cast to be a part of something larger than one individual or even one individual church.

- Even meeting in a temporary location, the church is experiencing new growth from salvation/baptism and will be poised financially to make a major impact on a new, growing part of the area.

Randy is currently the Editor of the Baptist Bible Tribune. He writes articles on church replanting and revitalization.

Maryann Stuart Executive Pastor of Warehouse Church, **Plano Texas**

1. Name(s) of your church—old and current:
    a. Old: First Baptist Church/ Aston, Pa
    b. New: Life Church/ Aston, Pa   --which joined with
    c. Old: Marcus Hook Baptist Church/ Linwood, Pa   -- and became
    d. New: Bridge Church/ Linwood, Pa
    e. Old: Canyon Creek Church/ Richardson ,TX
    f. New: Warehouse Church/ Plano, TX

2. How long have you been there?
    a. First Baptist Church/ three years   Life Church/ three years
    b. Marcus Hook Baptist Church/six months   Bridge Church/ two years
    c. Canyon Creek/ three years   Warehouse/ Since 2017

3. Would you say your church was dying—needing revitalization, or dead— needing resurrecting?
    a. Dead needing resurrecting

4. Without naming names, would you be able to describe major things that happened that led to your church's death or near-death experience?
    a. **First Baptist**: physically, emotionally, and spiritually dead.
    b. The finances were mismanaged, not living within the budget, and the pastor and family using the money for personal expenditures.
    c. There was no growth.
    d. No leadership.
    e. No vision or purpose. Just trying to survive each day.
    f. Very unhealthy school that needed to be shut down.
    g. **Marcus Hook**: physically and emotionally sick.
    h. Their building was neglected and their congregation was slowly dying off and getting smaller.
    i. They were not reaching people.
    j. Worship was outdated and not forward thinking.
    k. They just did everything because it was always done that way. Really no thought to why they were doing anything.

l. **Canyon Creek**: physically, emotionally, and spiritually dead.

m. The finances were mismanaged, they lived well beyond their means. Extravagant building and lavish spending, but way over budget and struggling to survive.

n. The staff did everything and the congregation just consumed.

o. No leadership, no vision, no growth and very immature people. Very inward thinking.

p. A long history of sexual sin, never addressed except to fire and hire.

q. Same was true in the school and the relationship was very unhealthy.

5. Can you describe a process that led to your church's breakthrough?

    a. The lead pastor, who came in to help the churches that I was part of, had a vision, a plan, and the leadership ability to make it happen. It needed someone with great communication skills and great compassion, to love people through the process but to be strong enough not to back down when God is directing a certain way.

    b. He helped the people understand what a healthy church should look like and lead in those changes. Having a vision that people can see, and really drawing and communicating that picture for them in steps is important.

6. What are some health indicators you can measure in your church (vital signs of life)?

    a. Growth.

    b. Salvations increasing.

    c. Baptisms.

    d. New members being added.

    e. A vision.

    f. A plan.

    g. Leadership strong and in place.

    h. Accountability on all levels.

    i. Growing leaders.

    j. Healthy and growing volunteers.

    k. Increased giving.

    l.   An excitement that's contagious to those coming in for the first time.

7. How can you make sure that when it is time to move on (retire, call time of death) that you will be leaving your church healthy for next generation?

    a. In my area on staff, I would make sure that those I have taking my place are equipped and trained with everything they need to succeed and take their ministry to the next level and so they feel confident in their role.

    b. I would want them to understand the vision, but also know how to take the vision that's in place to the next level and make the vision their own to grow even more.

Maryann has served with me since 2008 in Philadelphia, then came with me to Dallas in 2015. She started as our Children's Pastor, then did Life Groups-assimilation, and now is my Executive Pastor, CFO, and manages our Administration Team.

Pastor Tim Chambers *Fresh Start Church,* **Egg Harbor Township, NJ**

1. Name (s) of your church—old and current:

    a. Old: Trinity Baptist Church

    b. Old: Shore Fellowship Church

    c. New: Fresh Start Church

2. How long have you been there? Since 2001

3. Would you say your church was dying—needing revitalization, or dead—needing resurrecting?

    a. Dying Needing Revitalization.

4. Without naming names, would you be able to describe major things that happened that led to your church's death or near-death experience?

    a. I would say that the Congregational Rule structure of the church was a huge cause of its condition.

    b. The three previous Pastors before I was called had moral failures.

5. Can you describe a process that led to your church's breakthrough?

    a. On September 9, 2001 we had a Church Discipline meeting that was, no doubt, make or break for the church. As a result of that meeting, we were able to change the structure of our church to a Pastoral-led model that allowed us to be set up for success and growth instead of control.

6. What are some health indicators you can measure in your church (vital signs of life)?

    a. Percentage of first-time guest weekly.

    b. Percentage of returning guests.

    c. Level of those who are Engaged in our Journey Groups.

    d. Giving.

    e. Serving.

7. How can you make sure that when it is time to move on (retire, call time of death) that you will be leaving your church healthy for next generation?

    a. Honestly, you just have to set up a structure that allows for a transition and not a transplant. Many churches aren't considering what's next, and as a result they just parade Pastor after Pastor through the church with a completely different vision every time. This causes confusion and often competing vision.

Fresh Start Church runs 1300 in four weekend services at one location. Pastor Tim is a leader in C3 Global Network, influencing thousands of pastors all over the world.

Survey Observations:

Pastor Brian Moore of CrossPointe in Anahiem California started a Facebook page for pastors in revitalization projects to come together in a forum and talk about individual journeys, encourage one another, and, for me, learn not to repeat mistakes. There are some great statistical differences and similarities from each pastor.

One encouraging and challenging take-away for me, personally, was that the churches that were experiencing exponential growth were with leaders that had been in their churches for 12 years or longer. I have to guard my heart against ministry envy. There are many pastors who have bigger churches and a larger scope of ministry. While my flesh wants to be the top dog, I constantly have to remind myself that my calling is not someone else's calling. I have visited and spoken in the churches of most of these pastors. Their facilities, demographics, socio-economic structure, and unchurched people in their communities are vastly different. They have different personalities, leadership skills, and a personal calling from God that I am not called to copy. The idea is to learn from each other without becoming each other!

I am also pleased to have the opinion of my Executive Pastor, Maryann Stuart, in this section. I needed an administrative, organized leader to help keep me on the right path without compromising value systems or a blameless lifestyle. Maryann Stuart is a perfect fit for my gift set and style of ministry. She does not preach on Sundays, but she does help me prepare my whole team for the most important day of the week, Sunday! Therefore, her perspective of our journeys is significantly important for this study.

Chapter 5

To B, or Not To B?

Believe it or not, one of my favorite classes that I took at Baptist Bible College was a mini-semester class taught by Professor Barbara Dell called, "Shakespeare." It was a literature elective that I signed up for reluctantly, but it truly was an excellent class. I am naming this chapter with a Shakespearean reference, then quoting him; Mrs. Dell would be very pleased.

> *"What's in a name? That which we call a rose by any other name would smell as sweet."* —Romeo.

In Chapter 4, I shared findings from a handful of pastors about their revitalization or resurrection church project. There were things that were unique about each church, but also some things in common. One glaring common decision made by each church is that they changed their name, and specifically, the churches that had "Baptist" in their name dropped it in their new name. This is not as controversial as it was 15-20 years ago, but it still has divided many pastors and churches from other churches, colleges, and even denominations or fellowships.

The purpose of this chapter is to give some idea and understanding to the "why" this decision was made. I cannot speak for every church that has done this, or even every pastor and church that I interviewed. I can, however, speak into the motives of our last two churches (The Bridge Church and Warehouse Church) that God resurrected from the dead.

The evolution of the name for The Bridge Church had a longer journey with extra steps. We were leading First Baptist Church (FBC) in Aston, PA. We called the Time of Death for FBC and renamed it LIFE Church. LIFE Church merged with Marcus Hook Baptist Church, and we reorganized and renamed it The Bridge Church.

At the time we renamed FBC to LIFE Church, FBC was the only Baptist church in that community. The money trouble and division among the leaders were the two leading causes of the church having a very poor reputation in the community. I invited someone to our church early in my tenure at FBC and the response spoke into the negative reputation the church had in the community, "that Baptist church is full of crooks." I hate to share this, but it was not an exception, it was the reputation of the church.

The new name was necessary because of the name we were trying to make famous, Jesus Christ. This is not meant to sound pious or self-righteous. One of our seniors in the church, Dotty McKelvey, suggested the change, to the dismay of some of our other seniors, and said "If you want to build a new reputation than you need a new name altogether." She also said "The important thing is that people know it is a church."

This was a breakthrough for our church which resonated with our body. To be very literal, the Baptist label is never mentioned in the Bible, of which I am sure every reader of this manuscript is very aware. The Baptist History and distinctives we have are very significant to our faith and church polity today, but I'll ask again, "What's in a name?"

Salvation is found in no one else, for there is no other NAME under heaven given to mankind by which we must be saved. Acts 4:12

I believe that everyone reading this would agree with the principle of the name of Jesus being significantly more important than the name of Baptists. We had the same reputation issue with Marcus Hook Baptist Church as we did with Canyon Creek Baptist Church. We were attaching self-inflicted injuries to the bride and the reputation of its bridegroom because the churches lost the right to use the former name.

A new beginning and rebranding were essential to the future and health of the church. I wonder how many churches that have contemplated changing or updating their name but decided not to, due to the great testimony and reputation the church had in their community.

My name is Edward Martin Trinkle, Junior. My dad told me on many occasions, "Don't do something stupid that will damage both of our names and reputation," as I was named after my dad, Edward, Sr. He would also tell me, "You could ruin a lifetime of great character with one bad decision."

Many churches that have needed revitalization or resurrecting have made this difficult decision because of this situation. I can only speak for the church boards that I have worked with and state emphatically, it was about a establishing a new name to start a new testimony.

I have observed that most people that get upset about this are other people who claim to be a Baptist. I think the world doesn't care one way or another, and I do not think that an unchurched or unsaved person would not consider a new church because of that name. The only people in my years of pastoring that have stated to me that they were looking for a Baptist church was people from other Baptist churches. We loved when people moved into our area and found our church because of our name. It was one less barrier to get them connected to our local body.

I think this argument needs to be contextualized and put under the microscope of today's culture and, as always, the Word of God. For years the only way to identify the church that was on the corner in your neighborhood was the sign outside of the church that had your name on it. Your name on your sign was the only way people knew who you were before they entered. Later came the church sign with interchangeable letters. You could put verses on these signs, dates for special days, and even clever quips so your community would think you were relational or a super conservative separatist church. The communication of who a church is and what it is about was revolutionized with the internet. We do a survey for our first-time guests. The one question that is almost unanimously "YES," is did you search for us online or look at our website? Most church websites have a "who we are" and even a "what we believe" icon that can be clicked on, letting you know more about that church than you would if it were just a Baptist church.

There was another dynamic in the Northeast, specifically at Marcus Hook Baptist Church. MHBC was started as an American Baptist Church. MHBC was not in compliance with the recent denominational practices. When we presented the merger idea to a very old, conservative congregation, they jumped all over it. They had waited out of fear but were eager to put a new name in place. We also place a very high value on being an INDEPENDENT, autonomous, and self-governing local church. What our local body needed to do was done for our community and our reputation. We also made sure to put a lot of information about our church on our website.

I am sure that every pastor I interviewed, and many others that have led their churches to make this decision, could give you many more reasons than I did for our "why." When we were putting together our purpose statement, which is:

"Building Lives, Strengthening Families, and Delivering Hope,"

We wanted our name to reflect a place where people felt welcomed, not judged, something unique that people would remember, and a name that would make our website easy to remember while also connecting it to the church name.

The omission of the word Baptist was not done by our board because we are not identifying with Baptist Distinctives, and we are not disassociating from nor are we mad at the BBFI, Southern Baptist Convention, or John the Baptist himself! I think the question that every church needs to ask themselves when they do a makeover with a revitalization, or a do-over with a resurrection project is, "what do I need to do to be most effective in sharing the gospel?"

I think it is Biblical to have a do whatever it takes mentality with getting people to Jesus. Luke 5:17-39 tells the story of the four friends who lowered their friend through a roof to get him to Jesus. They butted in line, broke social protocol, dismantled and possibly destroyed part of a roof, and bypassed the Pharisees to get their friend to the feet of Jesus. I think we need to worry less about what other Christians think about our churches and worry more about what the world thinks. As a church, we decided to spend less time pleasing the already convinced and pouring our resources and energy into people that do not know Him yet.

Here is the beauty of all of this. Church autonomy, an Independent Baptist Church distinctive, means we believe that a local church is a self-governing, self-sufficient, called out, local body of believers. I have pastor friends that have a different philosophy of outreach and different convictions with conservative methodology. We can celebrate each other without being divisive or judgmental. We focus on the unchanging and non-negotiables with our ministry partners. One value we have as a church is not to spend more time talking about what we are against, than what we are for.

The issue really isn't the "big B" or "little b" of being a Baptist, the issue is whether I am a brawler or a peacemaker among the brethren! Warehouse Church exists to lead people to become devoted followers of Jesus Christ, by *Building Lives, Strengthening Families, and Delivering Hope.*

Chapter 6

Let me Pump You Up!
Signs of Physical Health in a Local Church

Weekday morning TV shows tell you on Monday that Americans are obsessed with physical health. They feed into the premise throughout the show with different segments devoted to cooking healthy, 10-minute workouts, workout clothing, and the top 10 most affordable gyms in your city. The irony is that, on Tuesday, they will have 5 segments on holiday meals, the evil of body shaming, and choosing the best wines for your meals. We really are a country of extremes when it comes to health. There are people that are workout fanatics, while others are some of the most obese people in the world. I want to submit to you six signs of physical health in your local New Testament Church. We talked about vital signs in earlier chapters. This is a practical application of this idea for the church.

There is a clear consistent message spoken of throughout the church

You get visitors in the door, then in the auditorium, and they are listening. They listen to the music, the prayers, the announcements, the message, and they listen to what the kids learned. Your guests may even listen to some messages on podcast or Facebook to learn more about what they heard. Is your message clear? Do the teaching, preaching, youth services, children's services, small groups, and one-on-one discipleship lessons all give a clear presentation of the life changing gospel message of Jesus Christ? Does the church preach and teach the Bible, or does it use the Bible to support issues that are discussed? Is the personality of its leader(s) the focal point, or does the church clearly lift up the name of Jesus Christ? Does the church talk about the trinity of God, biblical authority, and the need for salvation? If you attend and you are not sure what the church's message is, that is a sign of poor health.

Are the conversations about the church positive?

There are many places the church is talked about, let's consider some of these so you can gauge whether or not your church is having heathy conversations. When anyone speaks from the stage; pastor, associate, prayer, worship pastor, or announcements guru, are they speaking into the health of the church or are they talking about how bad or hard things are? If you were a first-time guest, would you sense health or trouble? When people are in the halls after services, are there mouth-covering whispers with sadness being displayed, or are people laughing and staying long after services are over? Do life groups or small groups center around complaints and gossip, or is the conversation uplifting and honoring? Do staff meetings talk about people problems or growth initiatives? Are board meetings filled with reports of potential, initiatives, and planning, or reactions to mistakes that continue? What do people in the community think or say about your church? What is the social media conversation about when it comes to your church, activities, staff, or challenges? Is the messaging positive or a gossip ring? Here is a tougher personal question for pastors and church leaders: Do you talk to your friends in different areas about how much you love your church, or do you wish God would move you? Last but not least, what does the conversation about the church sound like in your home? Matthew tells us that out of the abundance of the heart the mouth speaks. What people say about your church publicly and privately speak into its physical health condition.

Does your church have a "staff" infection?

A "staff" infection is when one of the staff members of the church or their spouses, family members, or even children, speak negatively about the leaders, other team members and its church members. I know many pastors that have kept staff members too long in fear of what the church membership would think. There is no disloyal staff member worth keeping on your team, no matter how great they sing or how many people they are bringing to church. If they are personal-kingdom builders and are not loyal, they need to go. Churches need a clear hiring and firing process that the body understands. A sidenote to this would be if you let someone go, get in front of the story. If they are disloyal, they will talk about it, so you better give the right information to the right people. Unhealthy leaders and unhealthy churches tolerate unhealthy staff with bad behavior.

Does your church attract and keep first time guests; is your church growing?

This is semi-sensitive, but we are all adults, right? If your church is not exhibiting some form of growth, it is most likely unhealthy. Churches have cycles. I have pastor friends who lead churches in military towns and their turnover is part of the culture. This is an exception. Generally speaking, is your church attracting new people and keeping them? Are they leaving as fast as they come in, or is your church able to trace systematic positive growth over long periods of time? Growth equals signs of life and health, period.

Are your finances handled with care and transparency?

Money issues are usually an outward sign of much deeper issues. When you talk about money, are people sighing and rolling their eyes, or are they contemplating how they can grow in their faith and participate in the vision? Are your monthly and quarterly reports positive or in decline? Money challenges do not always mean things are on the downward turn, but it sure is a tangible way to speak into the health of your church.

Are your property, facilities, and church vehicles taken care of properly?

This is a bit of a pet peeve of mine. You don't have to have new things to know how to take care of them. You really do demonstrate your character and stewardship management by how you take care of what you have. If you are not grateful for what you have, it is usually demonstrated in the way you take care of your possessions and property. We have heard it said that God will not give you more until you can take care of what you have. Sometimes, God just wants to see you take care of what you have to demonstrate your gratefulness to Him.

How can I turn the health around in my church in these areas?

1. Speak a clear message about who God is and who your church is and keep it consistent throughout the entire church.

   Plan your series, know where you are going, and where the Lord wants to take the church. Talk with your key leaders about curriculum and directional statements and agendas. The church should be flowing the same direction at every level. It will not happen by accident without training, preparing, and verifying the results! We are_____, We talk about _____!

2. Keep the conversations about your church positive.
   This starts with leaders and their families; we must keep it positive, even during challenging times. Honesty always prevails but be careful not to be a "Negative Nelly" all of the time. Most churches with negative people having negative conversations reflect negative leadership. This starts at home with our spouses, moves into the staff meeting, right into the boardroom, and then from the pulpit!

3. Spend time with and train your staff, and deal with problems in a proper manner. You are going to hire a dud someday, that is a lock. How you handle this poor performer says more about your leadership than it does the person you need to let go. Be honest, be fair, control the conversation, be generous when they leave, sign non-disclosure agreements, and make sure you have good legal counsel for really difficult situations. Remember this, they don't always come bad, and if they turn out bad, they may be an honest reflection of you. We must train, disciple and build people. If you want a culture that has loyal staff, be loyal to them. Keep your word with salary commitments. Find ways to affirm and reward good behavior, not just critique bad performance.

4. Work on bringing and keeping visitors.
   Do you plan events and communicate your calendar so that a church novice understands what you are doing? If you're speaking in that Christian code language, visitors will not feel welcomed. Do not assume people understand you, over-communicate. Put together a great assimilation plan and get the right people to implement. People need to know you want them there. You need to communicate with both quality and clarity to get them back. I highly recommend Nelson Searcy's book *Fusion—Turning First-Time Guests into Fully Engaged Members of Your Church*. This will not happen by accident!

5. Hire a CPA, or a licensed bookkeeper and get people that know what they are doing with the Lord's money.
    PROTECT YOURSELF from making bad mistakes. Say this with me, the church's money belongs to the Lord! There are great templates for handling church finances. Here are a few easy to implement initiatives:

    •   Two signatures on every check.

    •   More than one person counts the money.

    •   Recording and reporting of money received and spent.

    •   Get help from a professional, and do things right.

    •   If they are not right, fix them today.

    •   Spend less than you receive.

    •   Make a budget and stick to it.

6. Take care of your property, all of it!
7. Again, this is as much a part of stewardship as handling money. Hire great help, or recruit and train great volunteers to take care of your grounds, buildings, and vehicles. Even though it is not yours, treat it like it is! A clean van, with up-to-date oil changes and records will show your church you take care of the Lord's property and you can be trusted. When buildings and vehicles are in decline, you can be sure they are factors leading families to leave the church. I love asking retirees to take care of our church vehicles because they know how to! When you use vehicles for activities, expect them returned clean and ready for the next trip. Honor God by honoring and taking care of what is His! This is the pathway to trust and future blessings.

These are simple steps, but they will speak into your church's level of physical heath!

Ed Trinkle

Chapter 7

Tell me about your childhood... Is Our Church Emotionally Healthy or Unhealthy?

The idea of emotional health carries a bit of a tone of Freudian teaching regarding modern psychology. I picture a patient on the counselor's couch and the therapist asking, "Can you tell me about your childhood?" The presupposition is that someone hurt you or negatively influenced you to be emotionally unhealthy today. Everyone has a past and carries emotional baggage; that all started with sin back in the Garden of Eden. I wonder how many times, after the fall, did Adam and Eve fight about what happened, or carry emotional baggage because of it?

The idea that churches suffer with an unhealthy emotional environment is not a difficult principle to understand since churches are filled with emotionally unhealthy people. I want to submit seven areas in which churches suffer from emotional instability, and then offer some hope of how to achieve emotional stability in your local body of Christ.

Emotional Instability Marker #1: When the church values tradition over truth.

There are many examples of this type of instability in the gospels. John 1:11 states that Jesus, "*...came unto His own, and His own did not receive Him.*" This could be an argument of how Jesus could become emotionally unstable. Since we know that He did not, we understand the verse is referring to people who were in the presence of Jesus, as self-proclaimed representatives of God, and they did not recognize Jesus. What happened in the lives of these Pharisees that caused them to be blind to the coming of the Son of God? They were not looking for Jesus, they were too busy worrying about who was looking at them, while they were focused on looking at themselves. They valued their garments, position, and perceived influence over the thought of the Messiah being in their midst. I want to refer to an article written by church consultant Carey Nieuwhof, in which he submits seven signs that Pharisees are running your church.

Leaders like to show themselves off

Everyone thinks they are better than everyone else

There is a "love of money" issue

There is too little compassion

Leaders expect others to do what they don't do

No one is closer to God

Leaders are jealous when others get "their" attention

When we become the priority, we lose sight of our mission to draw people to Christ. Are we so busy promoting ourselves, that people do not even know we are trying to draw them to Jesus? We also need to be aware of doing things in our churches that focus on the people inside and forget about the people outside our walls. Many churches get stuck: stuck in methods, stuck in traditions, and stuck on themselves. I had a member of our church in Philadelphia ask if we could put a committee together to make sure there is accountability with the idea of keeping members happy. I told him to lead a group (I'm not a fan of committees) of people to put a plan together on how the church could connect to and make our community happy as we are their neighbors. There are modern day Pharisees that represent emotional instability.

Emotional Instability Marker #2: We give with the wrong motives.

What is driving the community of your church to give regularly? Jesus talks about money and possessions throughout the Gospels. Consider the Pharisee who wanted everyone to know he was giving sacrificially with an ostentatious display of giving an offering to the Lord; Jesus said the attention and the gasps he received were the extent of his reward.

Wrong motive #1: Giving to draw attention to self.

We promote systematic giving in our church in multiple ways: envelopes, online giving, text giving, ACH giving, and we have offering boxes in the back of our auditoriums. This negates much of the "visible" nature of passing the offering plate. But it must be pointed out that posting about your generous gift on Facebook then negates that original discretion!

Wrong motive #2: Giving out of guilt or duty.

There is a tendency to hit those heart strings to open the purse strings. There is nothing wrong with helping the hungry or poor, we are supposed to, but not because we feel guilty. Churches need to be careful not to say or do things that promote guilt giving. If the motivation is penance, or making up for personal failures, our giving is not for the right reason. We also have to be careful that our giving doesn't become just another one of our bills like our electric bill or car payment. We're giving to *God* and His work!

Wrong Motive #3: Giving to gain or control.

There is another motive that people give to the church, which is to get attention of the leaders to influence decisions. They are giving to gain. The truth is money can be a big influence, and churches need money to do ministry. I have personally dealt with affluent members who let me know what they were giving to persuade leadership with preferences. Sometimes the initiative that they want support for is not a bad one but using their financial position to get there is unethical.

Emotional Instability Marker #3: The church has a critical, judgmental spirit.

I referenced a book a few chapters ago called, *Antagonists in the Church*. Like many pastors, I could give story after story about people who are just contrarian about everything. I remember that I was getting ready to walk into our second service one Sunday morning, when one of our senior ladies, we will call her Ann, came up to me screaming, "You are a liar!"

I asked her… what I lied about and asked her to watch her tone.

She yelled… even louder, "You promised us traditional music in the first service; this music is rock and roll. You are a liar!"

I replied… "Ann, you are at the second service, an hour late for the first service. We had a sweet time in the early service, not one complaint today, until now."

I also approached her husband and told him that if she ever addressed me like that in public again, I would ask her to leave the church. We would have one more confrontation in a business meeting, about a month later. She and her husband went on and on about individual salaries, the building project we were in, and missionary support. I was ready for the meeting and pulled up their giving records; they were giving about $25 per month, far from a tithe, and not even on a regular basis. I said, "Sir, you are not asking questions, you're making statements. I'd like for you to wait until the end of my presentation, and at that time we will take questions from members who tithe regularly."

We had another member ask if we could put up a suggestion box and held up a miniature plastic church with a coin slot on the top. This miniature church was something you would see in Kid's Church for coin offerings. He asked if we could use it for suggestion or complaints, so that people with an issue would not be embarrassed to share publicly, and they could make these suggestions anonymously. I kindly told the man that I would be happy to meet with anyone who was unhappy in my office with one of our board members. I also told him there was a big green box in the parking lot we would use for anonymous suggestions (I was referring to the dumpster). When people complain about everything, they are carrying hurt that they are not talking about and lashing out. When churches facilitate or enable chronic complainers, the church is emotionally unhealthy.

Emotional Instability Marker #4: The church body communicates a victim mentality.

We love to blame others for bad circumstances, as much as we like to communicate the fact that we are victims of someone else's mistakes or hurt. Each one of the churches we have pastored had an Eeyore—Woe is me, I've been wounded by leadership, circumstances, whatever, and it is *not fair.*

Pain is real, and hurt sometimes comes from other people, but if our message is only describing how others have hurt us, we are questioning the sovereignty of God in our lives. This also happens when there is a failure in the leadership; victims blame what they are not doing on those that hurt them or messed up.

Emotional Instability Marker #5: It's someone else's turn to serve, I've done my time.

I like to call this, "Been there/done that-itus." George Barna claims in his book entitled, *Revolution*, that Christians on average, will serve the Lord fervently for about five years before they tinker out. There are a few circumstances that cause us to burn out: We observe what others are not doing, we think we are working harder than those who are being paid, we have personal circumstances in our life that are distracting us, and we get hurt by others who serve.

Emotional Instability Marker #6: The church has turned into a memorial of the past.

We tend to put more value in things than we do in people. When you have been part of a church for a long time, it can represent a very stable force in your life. We change jobs, move, and get old, but there is that amazing church that we have been a part of for so many years. We try to preserve furniture, traditions, rooms, music, and methods, forgetting that they are simply tools to help us reach and minister to *people*. Our church in Marcus Hook had a radio station on AM radio that they had been using to broadcast the church services live for over 60 years. It was the longest continuous running church service on the radio in the United States. The church was so proud of the program. They loved the service being on the radio when they were sick, or weather was bad. They did not want it to reach families, however, they wanted it for themselves. When we introduced online giving to our church in Dallas, the deacons voiced their negative feelings on it because they could not see who was giving anymore. They were busybodies and were keeping track of envelopes and amounts. Be aware when your congregation talks more about the past than it does the future.

Emotional Instability Marker #7: We protect our "areas."

I was visiting a church in middle Pennsylvania on a Sunday night on our way to youth camp. We went into the auditorium and there were seat cushions everywhere. I asked one of the ushers what they were for, and he said, "So no one sits in their seats." I laughed because I thought he was kidding. He was not kidding!

Our church in Marcus Hook also had a library with commentaries and old paperback books. They said they wanted it in the church lobby in case someone came in off the street to check out a Christian book. The only catch, though, you had to be a member to check out the book. Sometimes our stuff brings us comfort and great memories, the problem comes when we value stuff more than people.

How can we restore emotional health in our church?

Three books were primary influences on our journey of revitalization and resurrection at the churches where we ministered: *Autopsy of a Dead Church*, *Breakout Churches*, and *I am a Church Member*. These three books were all authored by Thom Rainer. I have read all three books more than once, as did my staff and leadership teams. One board member told me after reading *Autopsy of a Dead Church*, that it was too much because it was all true.

Steps to Restoring Emotional Health

Restoring emotional health to your church must happen the way true recovery starts for a person with emotional sickness. You must admit you are sick and get some help. It is very sad, but there are churches that have been in decline for years, have disjointed bodies, rarely have people saved, but think they are healthy. We love to repeat the verse in Matthew 16:18, "....*I will build My church and the gates of Hell will not prevail against it.*" We use that verse as a disclaimer for the unhealthy status of our church. I think a crude example of this is an extremely overweight person who drinks diet coke, thinking they are making healthy decisions. It takes more than a diet soda to lose weight, it also takes more than a name on the door or a good sermon to make a church healthy.

STEP ONE: The leaders must acknowledge the unhealthy emotional state of the church.

I am not speaking directly into the kind of structure your church should or should not have. Whatever leadership structure you have in place, it starts with this group. This is easier said than done, because our pride keeps us from admitting we need help. If we admit we need help, we are in some way admitting we have failed or are failing. If the church is pastor- led, like our church is, it starts with him. This is a big, scary step, but it is freeing because, while being unhealthy is a burden, failing to do anything about it is deadly.

I am the kind of person who needs to psyche himself up to get on a scale, but it was a necessary step to making some critical decisions to turn my life around. Physically, I had to look at a scale, look at a mirror, and admit to myself it was time to change. I then had to take the first step of getting help, submitting to a plan, surrounding myself with positive influences, workout, and stick to the plan. It seems simple, but again, we live in one of the unhealthiest, most obese countries in the world. Simple doesn't mean easy.

It seems simple for churches to do the same with emotional sickness. But it can be very difficult to admit you are sick and get help. However, when you understand there is a reason for the unhealthy diagnosis of your church, and admit you need to change, you know some changes are imminent.

STEP TWO: Strategically communicate and get buy-in from the church.

This is the step that takes the most emotional work, so be ready for some push back. We have stood before our church announcing changes, initiatives, transition steps, sale of property, and even death, and we've learned you have to be prayed-up and unified when you stand before your people. It is recommended to have some meetings with key families, first, and use your pulpit time to speak into the need for the church to be healthy. When you do stand before the people, do not bash or blame anyone. Paint a picture of what a healthy church looks like. You do not need to compare your church to others to do this. Give biblical principles of what a sick church looks like and what a healthy church looks like, then state your case, and the steps you intend to take to get there.

This is a critical time in the life of the pastor and the board. This could split a church or cause some serious attrition. Our church in Dallas went from averaging 400 in December of 2016 to starting The Warehouse Church 7 months later with 94 people. This is a kick in the pants on your pride if you are not prepared. We never wanted anyone to leave. We were surprised by some that left and surprised with some who stuck it out. We developed the mantra of: Life looks much clearer through a windshield than a rear-view mirror. Thom Rainer says in *Autopsy of a Dead Church*, "The church must be willing to make some radical changes."

STEP THREE: GET SOME HELP!

My shameless plug for my personal health journey is the help I received from Dr. Brian Hooten, of Hooten Chiropractic and Wellness Center. The coaching, encouragement and accountability I received from his staff, and him personally, changed my life, and the health of my entire family. Pastor and church leaders, it may be time to bring in a fresh voice or influence.

This does not mean it is necessary to fire your current pastor, call for the resignation of your board, or fire your staff. Hire a consultant. Take your time and hire the RIGHT CONSULTANT. This does not mean you have to Google, "transitioning your church consultants!" You can do some homework and put a small team together from your pastoral staff or board to find someone that will help you. Be smart and plan properly. My dad used to tell me, "Poor planning produces poor product." I am sure he did not make this up, but it is where I heard it. Proper research and planning can include these steps:

Talk to your denominational leaders who know your church and understand your need.

Talk to some churches that have gone through this, that are not out of your reach financially or in capacity. For instance, you probably do not need a pastor who leads a church of 6000 if you're transitioning or revitalizing a church of 500. The next level leader may be a pastor or staff pastor who leads 700-1000 people and can help you plan your health track accordingly.

Do some reading together. There are tremendous resources for helping churches revitalize. There is a list of books in the bibliography section of this book that I highly recommend.

Get some help from non-church entities. We sought legal counsel, real estate advice from a realtor outside of our church, a Certified Public Accountant, a commercial realtor in leasing market, architects, and general contractors. We have to be smart enough to know that we need help from people smarter than we are in specific fields. I even talked to a grief counselor to understand how to minister to people who would take the change very hard and personally.

PASTORS: Get support from other pastors who have done this. It's hard! You will question your calling, your competence, and sometimes your sanity. You know all of the statistics we read about guys who quit ministry or fail. A lot of those stories happen right as things get difficult in your church. Satan hates what Jesus loves—the Church and will attack His representatives—shepherds and leaders of the Church, so he can destroy it. We are not built to do life and ministry alone.

STEP FOUR: Communicate and Work Your Plan.

Communicate, don't complicate. Know where you are, where you are going, and how you are going to get there. Your communication should include updates celebrating victories and affirming the committed when there are setbacks. It will happen but do your best to avoid people accusing you of under-communicating. Like I said, it's going to happen, and you have to be ready for this. We had a critical business meeting for our church announcing the sale of the building. We voted six months previously to sell it and we were sharing with the church that it sold. We put it in the bulletin two weeks before the meeting, as required by our by-laws. We announced it at the end of each service. We posted on our website and on the church Facebook page, sent a mass text alert to every cell phone on file, and sent an email letting people know the dates. We still had some antagonists accuse us of pushing this through and under-communicating. It takes physical, emotional, and spiritual strength to persevere. Stay with your plan. When you second-guess yourself, do it to your buddies, not publicly. Stay strong. If the Lord is leading you to do this, He will give you the resources, encouragement, and strength to complete the work.

STEP FIVE: You've got to pray just to make it today!

The effective, fervent prayer of a righteous man means a lot! (James 5:16). Your time alone with God will determine the success of the plan and process. This does not guarantee it will be easy. Mark Batterson wrote this in his book called *Circle Maker*:

Bold prayers honor God, and

God honors bold prayers.

God is not offended by your

Biggest dreams and boldest prayers.

He is offended by anything less.

If your prayers

Aren't impossible to you,

They are insulting to God.

"Now to him who is able to do immeasurably more than all we ask or imagine, according to his power that is at work within us."
Ephesians 3:20

When you go to a doctor and he/she tells you to eat less sugar, eat more vegetables, exercise regularly, and take some vitamins, you are probably not blown away by this information. I think what some of our spiritual disciples have communicated can have the same impact. We make it harder than it needs to be. We want God to heal the church that He gave His life for. Some daily conversation asking for guidance, strength, resources, wisdom, and patience just seems like the obvious thing to do. Call a prayer warrior, and more importantly, become one.

The emotional health of the church will reflect the emotional health of its leaders. Consider the similarities and differences in preparing for a battle and a war. For a battle, you need a plan, an objective, the proper supplies, the right number of soldiers, great leaders—and do not forget about the weapon(s) you need to defeat the enemy. To win a war, you have to be ok with losing a battle. We must keep our eyes focused on the Objective and minimalize casualties.

I was reading about some of the turn-around battles of World War 2. When General Eisenhower was meeting with the Allied Forces leaders, they put an aggressive plan together to invade Normandy Beach. The had to estimate number of soldiers needed, supplies, artillery, planes, ships, and vehicles. They sent some to Normandy and Osage Beach by ship and U-Boat, and some through paratroopers. They also had to make a morbid estimate of how many soldiers would die in this invasion. They had to consider the cost.

For the revitalization of a church, the restoration of physical and emotional health is a high risk / high reward endeavor. The cost is not our membership role numbers, our income from offerings, some staff, or key church people. The cost was the blood of Jesus Christ. He paid for this church, and He expects us to keep it healthy!

Chapter 8

Spiritual Death of a Church and The Pathway to Resurrection

Jesus said to her, "I am the resurrection and the life. The one who believes in me will live, even though they die. John 11:25

There is a way that appears to be right, but in the end it leads to death. Prov 14:12

We have talked about why it happens, how churches have been reborn because of it, but it just feels wrong to declare a church dead. God is the maker and sustainer of life, so who are we to be able to say whether or not a church is dead? We are certainly not declaring God dead, or Christianity dead. We are acknowledging that healthy life does not exist in that local assembly, and it is time to do something about it. The point of this whole manuscript is to lead to an understanding that the resurrecting power of Jesus Christ saves not only people but churches!

Causes of Death of a Local Church

Number 1: Disqualifying Sins

No discipline seems pleasant at the time, but painful. Later on, however, it produces a harvest of righteousness and peace for those who have been trained by it. Hebrews 12:11

One of the most visible causes of death in a local church is from a major moral failure by the lead pastor or key members of its leadership team. Carey Nieuwhof wrote a great article entitled: *"Five Reasons that Pastors Fail Morally."* The reasons were choosing isolation over community, no longer confessing sins, eliminating thought of consequences, ignoring the rules, and seeing failure as a way of escape (so it is premeditated). He wrote something interesting as a commentary about failures like this, "No one writes or prays with clean hands."

I have some very close friends that have suffered the consequences of personal moral failure. The truth is, this is an all too familiar subject anymore. It is pretty easy to react and take a position of high moral judgement when faced with the effects of this type of sin. Most pastors who understand how delicately we have to serve the Lord each day as His representatives remember what Jesus said in the book of Matthew, that looking at a woman lustfully is the same as committing adultery. I must agree with Nieuwhof's conclusion that no one is totally innocent. Jeremiah 17:9 tells us, *"The heart is deceitful above all things and desperately wicked, who can know it?"*

I believe the Bible is very clear about sin when it tells us in 1 John 1:9, we can have absolute forgiveness. The point is that our Father will forgive, but we still suffer the consequences of sin in our flesh. A moral failure is when we commit a sin that causes leaders to lose the trust of their people. These sins can include, but are not exclusive to, adultery, stealing money from the church, gossiping about members and leaders, using your position for personal gain, and leading the church to do wrong intentionally. I would say the first two, adultery and stealing, are what most of us think of as a moral failure. I know of churches that have forgiven and kept a lead pastor that committed adultery as well as churches that have overreacted when their pastor was seen at a public restaurant with another woman. The principle idea of a disqualifying moral decision would be an action (sin, of course) that would cause your members to lose trust in you.

Number 2: Long-Term Unconfessed Sin

"A little leaven leavens the whole lump…" Galatians 5:9

Sin can, and always does, have a catastrophic domino effect in the lives of people in its wake. We minimalize a "white lie," a strategic exaggeration, or even a quick look at pornography online, and forget that the entire human race has been born dead spiritually because Adam and Eve ate fruit from the wrong tree. If it were only that simple. The sin was disobedience, the consequence was known before the action was committed. This is so true with our sins today. Have you ever thought or talked to anyone who thought that an affair would not have consequences, or a sin that snowballs out of control would not have consequences?

In Nieuehof's article about why pastors fail morally, he states that some do it on purpose as a way out, implying the burden of carrying other sins that he had not confessed. Unconfessed sin is not always directed at one leader either. I believe one of the unconfessed sins of our church in Dallas was the removal of a pastor without just cause.

The pastor was not perfect, as none of us are, but the way this was handled haunted the church as the next pastor they called was living in immorality, during, and after his tenure as lead pastor.

Number 3: The Church Ceases to be the Church

The morality sins have the gasp factor and are pretty easy to pinpoint. What about the sin of not being the church we were called to be, spending the church's resources on things not connected to the mission of the church, not reaching people, not worshipping God, or just losing its way?

I went on a motorcycle tour through New England with a group of bike enthusiasts and it seemed that, in every town we would ride through, there would be a vacant church building, or a church building turned into an ice cream shop or town hall (literally). I asked a pastor familiar with these areas what caused these churches to close, so many in the region. He said they cared more about themselves than their communities and lost the right to be a church because they stopped *being* the church. We live in a post-modern society where Christianity and a Judeo-Christian ethic or moral code is no longer a standard. Simultaneously, churches are closing daily all over the United States. Thom Rainer states in *Autopsy of a Deceased Church* that 40% of the 150,000 churches in the United States are unhealthy or dying.

Number 4: There are no traceable signs of life.

There are some tangible signs of life that a healthy church will have; there are also indicators that a church is dying or dead. Thom Rainer gives six notable signs of a church that is extremely unhealthy or dead in *Autopsy of a Deceased Church*: The church has suffered numerical decline steadily over a long period of time; The church has been going through a long time of apathy, and intense conflict; The church is not known in the community, or even known to exist; More people are leaving the church than are joining the church; Frustration and conflict limit the times the staff and the lead pastor stay; and The past is the primary topic of conversation over the present or future.

Number 5: Unwillingness to accept help

I have been a lead pastor for 20 years and have counseled hundreds of people. I have had many people come to me looking for help, and also to tell me of someone in their life that needs help. I have been asked to contact husbands to discuss pornography addictions or infidelity issues by their wives, and the husbands had no idea their wife was asking me.

I tell people the only way I can talk to them is if they call me, and that they need to talk to the Lord to ask Him to get them help. This is the same principle for a dead church, you really cannot come in uninvited and express your concern over the church's health.

We don't look for help because of embarrassment, of being somewhat lazy, and because it is easier to avoid a conflict than to face it head-on. Christians can just be stubborn, and they are so used to the church being dysfunctional that they almost like it better that way because it is familiar. It is like having "Stockholm Syndrome" in the church.

Wouldn't it be wonderful to go back in time to when the disqualifying sin took place and stop it, or maybe go back and pick a different leader, or make a different decision? The fact of the matter for your church is that you know, and the leaders know, that the life of this church is over.

It is easy to get stuck in the blame game, or spend too much time mourning the situation you are in. The brawlers and antagonists may even want to keep fighting and complaining because that is what they do. When we discussed Time of Death in the first chapter, we also talked about death being part of God's plan. In John 11, Mary, Martha, and the crowd were disappointed and somewhat mad at Jesus for not getting to Lazarus in time to keep him from dying. Jesus told them this had happened so that God would be glorified and that people would believe in Him. Lazarus had to die so that Jesus could raise him from the dead. We cannot assume that God allowed the sin or was the Author of the apathy and hurt, but we do know that throughout scripture, God takes a mess and turns it into a message.

The need for the resurrection of a dead church is sad, even heartbreaking, but a beautiful story may be in the works. Something dead can be given new life. I think the resurrection of Canyon into Warehouse did not happen when we changed the name and did the legal work, but when we did the spiritual work. It happened when old things passed away and all things became new (2 Cor 5:17). It happened when we dealt with our past publicly. It happened when we asked the Lord to forgive our church. It happened when we asked the Lord to do what we could not do—raise the dead!

Funeral's Over – Now what?

What does the new or resurrected church look like? The time of death was called, the funeral is over. What are some steps churches can take into resurrection?

New Life Option Number 1: Replant the church

Replanting the church can be a great option for rebirth! This option requires a strong core of committed, giving members, and some resources for the relaunch. We were blessed with both when we closed Canyon Creek and launched Warehouse Church. The resources are needed to secure a place to meet, and to purchase the furniture and supplies needed. When we replanted in Philadelphia, we had very limited resources, but we were very creative at putting our mobile church supplies together. If you are replanting, it would be a great idea to do it under the aegis of a healthy church, or as part of a healthy church plant organization like Converge, Acts 29, or ARC. The coaching and resources that come with the connection to a healthy organization can be a great way to start anew.

Replanting can help you correct some of the mistakes of the former entity. You have the ability to establish fresh and potentially updated church governance to eliminate dysfunction and control. Warehouse Church had assistance from local churches, a Christian lawyer, and a church consultant. What a great privilege to establish a new work, a new reputation, and a new vision. This took some time and careful planning, but we started with physical, emotional, and spiritual health!

New Life Option Number 2: Merge with an existing healthy church.

Marcus Hook Baptist Church had a great property, but no leadership or capability to manage the property, let alone sustain a healthy ministry model. When MHBC merged with Life Church, they went from 60 in attendance to 660 in one week. They went from $2500 per week in income to $15,000 per week. There were some challenges that needed to be worked out, but Life brought life to this building, and life to this old church. I would suggest a new name and bylaws as part of the merge agreement or immediately after the merge takes place. You must have a plan for the assets to protect them. This can be tricky with dated bylaws or if the property is owned by a denomination. We had great advice from a consulting, supportive church to *secure legal advice*. This was a game changer to protect both bodies and the newly acquired property.

New Life Option Number 3: Give the building away.

It can be given to your denomination, to a heathy church in the area, or to a church-planting organization.

The assets are the church's and the church is the Lord's, so the assets need to be distributed with care towards a church, a church plant, or denomination that can establish a healthy work in the area. We have also worked with a church that closed, sold its property, and gave the financial proceeds to a church plant in a different community.

It is a great idea to have a denomination guiding this decision, or a church that would be willing to help close the business of the former work.

New Life Option Number 4: Give the building to a representational church.

By that I mean one that represents the demographics of the community.

In his book, *The Circle Maker*, Mark Matterson talks about his property acquisition from a former church that hadn't represented the changing demographics of the neighborhood. They were able to move to a new neighborhood and grow. Batterson's church refurbished the old church building and built a thriving new church in Washington DC.

When Lazarus rose from the dead, the name of the Lord became (more) famous. A new church, with enough disconnect from the old work, can start with a new name and new reputation. The new church brings energy, vitality and health. Maybe this was the plan all along for our church in Dallas. Maybe the church's life was supposed to go from 1972 to 2017. The ministry continues. The Warehouse Church is healthy and growing and becoming a force to be reckoned with in Plano, Texas. We started Warehouse Church with 94 people, and a year and a half later had 500 on Christmas weekend. Warehouse Church has only 20 people who came with us from the former Canyon Creek Church. Most of the members of Warehouse Church are new believers. As much as we are excited about our future, we are being careful not to repeat the mistakes of our past.

Chapter 9

If I Could Turn Back Time

I like putting a meme on my Facebook profile of Cher singing this song on Daylight Savings Time Sunday: The day we get an extra hour of sleep, my wife's favorite day of the year.

The past can be a very powerful influence in our lives. The past can also be a negative influence. We discovered that one of the reasons churches struggle so much today is because they spend so much time celebrating or lamenting over the past and rarely think about the present, let alone the future of the church. And when it comes to the past, it seems like humanity has some short-term memory loss.

Many Christian households decorate their homes with plaques of Bible verses. Joshua 24:15 is one of those verses often seen on the wall of a church office or home of a Christian family. "*But if serving the Lord seems undesirable to you, then choose for yourselves this day whom you will serve.......But as for me and my household, we will serve the Lord.*"

This is a powerful statement of a non-negotiable for Joshua and his family here in the last chapter of his book. The same passage tells us that "*all of Israel agreed with Joshua.*" Then in Judges 2, the children of Israel suffered from spiritual amnesia. Take a look at Judges 2:10:

"After that whole generation had been gathered to their ancestors, another generation grew up who knew neither the Lord nor what he had done for Israel."

The nation of Israel agreed with Joshua that they were going to love and serve the Lord exclusively, and they would not be influenced by neighboring countries and their idolatry. Reading in Judges we understand that the children and grandchildren of the Israelites that witnessed earth moving miracles, did not know the Lord or the great things that He has done.

One of two things happened, the parents or grandparents never taught their kids the great things that God had done for them, or the children and grandchildren choose to turn their backs on the Lord God of Israel. One way or the other, the nation of Israel suffered for many years, because they did not learn from their past.

The past is an interesting subject and unique for everyone. Two kids growing up in the same home, with the same parents, remember two distinct experiences. I have three siblings, two brothers and a sister. We remember great things about growing up, but we also carry hurt that is unique from each other. The past is a very powerful force and major influence in our lives.

This chapter is going to be about learning from and remembering the past in a negative way and in a healthy way. How you choose to view your past, and how the church chooses to view the past will determine your success or failure.

The past can have a negative impact on the church (and personal lives) because of both dysfunction and glory days. Your church does not need to have a mega-sin in its past, to make the influence of the past negative. If the church cannot live up to its past, the memory of a better time can be detrimental as well.

How does a church put the negative past behind? We had to do this with our church in Dallas. We had a funeral for our old church and asked God to forgive our body for allowing things to get as bad as they did. We had a spirit of sexual sin that was generational, as well as complacency, gossip, disrespect, and judgement. Many churches, ours being one, do not deal with sin that affects and infects the congregation. It is so much easier to just forget it, or deny it ever existed than it is to talk about and learn from it. Many times, it is even talked about with a critical spirit, from the pedestal of hypocrisy.

Major sin in the church's past that is never dealt with can turn into the very thing that limits the church and its potential. The church can put these negative impacting sins behind them by dealing with them publicly. Bring the sin before the church, teach on why it is sin from the Word of God, and ask the Lord to forgive the church.

We took communion after our forgiveness-seeking service, then prayed scripture about each sin over the church. The point is, you cannot leave a generational sin untreated. In 2 Kings 22, we find King Josiah reading scriptures that were forgotten about. He repented on behalf of the nation of Judah and instituted reform. He took the sins of his nation's past very seriously and made them right before God.

One of the difficult dynamics that we had to walk our church through is that most of the church did not know about the sexual sin habits of the past leaders, because the board had not dealt with it publicly. This must be handled delicately because you are dealing with people's lives, privacy issues, and the lawsuit culture we live in today. Be wise, be discreet, but don't bury it and hope it goes away.

The "glory days" can also haunt a church and have a negative impact on the present and future of the body. We had a self-appointed leader in The Bridge Church in

Philadelphia, that was a member of our pre-merge body of Marcus Hook Baptist Church. He wanted me to know that the church used to run 700, and how they did it, and why they needed to do things the same way even though the current church was in its 13th straight year of decline.

Our church in Texas also had people holding on to past memories and the glory days. Did you ever have a friend whose life was never the same after high school? They saw those years as the greatest days of their lives, and continued to talk about and relive them so much that it held them back in their future. Churches do this, they are afraid of change and a loss of identity. The worse argument in the world for continuing to do things the same way is "we have always done it that way." The best definition of insanity is, doing things the same way and expecting different results.

Using the past as an object lesson

I tell my church often that life is too short to be looking at it through your rear-view mirror. The past can hold you back if you dwell there; but if you totally forget about it, you can miss great learning opportunities for your future.

The bus ministry is something from the past that is not as relevant as it used to be. Many churches still have it because they always have and, back in the day, it was a cutting-edge philosophy because of the culture it was birthed from. In the 1950s and '60s people used mass public transportation to get everywhere. They bussed to work, to shop, to visit. Many American homes did not even have a car, let alone multiple cars.

The idea was to give people a free ride to church, a free bus ride. The very mode of transportation that cost them money to use during the week would be free to take them to church because the church cared and wanted to help. When this was happening, churches had fulltime bus pastors and mechanics, and many large churches had a fleet of busses. Families would ride to church together. This was genius and it worked.

But times changed. First, parents let their kids ride the same busses without them. Then buses were looked at as transportation for poor families. Now, days of the mega bus ministry are virtually non-existent in the United Stated. Holding to this as a ministry type has hurt churches. Using the principle of "let's do whatever it takes" to get people to church can be a great object lesson.

There are great lessons we have learned from sinful pasts, too, that had a big influence on things we did for our building. We put windows in every door to protect children and to protect reputations. We have rules about our pastoral staff meeting with and being alone with members of the opposite sex. We have rules about leaders taking children to the bathroom, and about having multiple teachers with kids at all times. There have been some horrific sins that have happened in churches across the United States. Once we deal with them and ask for forgiveness, we need to ask the Lord how we can learn from our mistakes and protect each other, the Lord's church, and the name of Jesus.

Honoring our Past

Our church, like many churches in the United States, honors its Veterans on Veterans Day weekend, and our fallen war heroes on Memorial Day Weekend. We honor our country on July 4th weekend, and Mothers and Fathers on their respective weekends. We do this because of the principle of honor. God honors honor. I tell my church that we honor UP, honor DOWN, and honor all around. Honor breeds honor in a church, as does dishonor.

Remembering and honoring is different than idolizing and regretting. There is nothing wrong with discontinuing a ministry in your church because it is irrelevant, or ineffective. It is not wrong to move from conservative, piano-driven, hymnal music to a full band with modern music. What is wrong about these things is how we do it. When we do it and dishonor the past, mock old ways, or have a condescending attitude towards things that our churches were built on, is not honoring to one another nor honoring to God.

We need monuments and memorials in our lives to remember the great things that God has done in our lives. God regularly instructed Israel to set up memorials as teaching tools for the next generations. Honoring people, and the past accomplishments, not only honors God, but it teaches the younger generation their responsibility to do the same. The important thing is to *use* the memorials to teach. They're not Atta-boy trophies to be put in a display case and forgotten, but markers pointing to what God has done, and can do again!

When it comes to the church, honor the right thing for the right reason. When we honor an anniversary, it is not our accomplishment, it is the Lords. When we dedicate a building or pay off a mortgage, is it not because of our accomplishments, but because of God's faithfulness and provision. The respect and honor that needs to be given to the church, should be directed to its Founder, our Lord Jesus Christ.

Considering church revitalization or a church resurrection, the past has a place for us to look back and learn and grow from it. We need to guard our hearts so that we are not repeating the sins of the past, and not dwelling in the glory days of the past. We do not have to hate our past to move on, nor do we want to be repeat offenders of its mistakes.

Physical, Emotional and Spiritual Health and The Past

We do something on our staff after a big day or big event. I ask our team to bring up two great things and one thing we could do better from the big day. I do twice as many positive because being overly critical is something we need to guard against. The takeaway being: what will we do again, and what can we do better? Break down your analysis of your past in the three main areas of this study, with the same exercise. I will walk through this exercise with Canyon Creek for Warehouse Church.

What are two great things from our past and one thing we could do better PHYSICALLY? The church had an excellent system for taking care of the finances. There had been money trouble in the past and the church learned from it and put safeguards in place to protect the church. The church had a great Chief Financial Officer and they did annual audits with good accountability to the board. The church was very willing to spend money to help missionaries and church planting projects. When the church had missions money they were ready to release it to help other ministries, when it did not, the people responded well to the plea.

The church could have been better about prioritizing the conversations in business meetings. We over-emphasized balance sheets and money. This is not to say that these things were not important, but they became the focus. The members saw it as their responsibility to watch over the money, and the pastor should just build the church. It was out of balance and zero trust existed. This was due to mistakes made in the past that the church never fully recovered from.

What are two great things from our past and one thing we could do better EMOTIONALLY?

The church was very good at taking care of its members. When people were in the hospital, they were visited, prayed for, and their family was looked after. The church loved their senior citizens and had a great ministry for them. They traveled, ate, went to the homes of one another, and genuinely care for each other.

There are always two sides of a coin and these two areas were great, but out of balance. The church became very inwardly focused and only cared about what was happening in our midst and was totally disconnected to the community. The church was also getting older, and while they valued the senior's ministry and doing things the "old way," they also lamented that their children were not attending church with them and blamed it on the church, which they wanted to control. It was an exercise in futility.

What are two great things from our past and one thing we could do better SPIRITUALLY?

The church valued the importance of teaching and preaching the word of God. The services, Sunday School Classes, children's and youth ministry were all biblically centered, and its teaching was a priority. The church loved it when people were saved and wanted to see this happen more. They could not understand why it did not happen more, but when it did they celebrated it.

The church should have dealt with the sin issues of its leaders openly. This was the primary reason the members did not respect or follow leaders well. The leaders were not trusted, and this culture of disrespect and not following leadership would be part of the church's demise. A church consulting firm, Injoy, told me it takes five years for a church to fully follow and trust a pastor after he is called. He also said it takes five to ten years to overcome the failure of the previous pastor, and that the failures stay with the position for that period of time.

A Blast from the Past

It is highly recommended that this study provokes you not only to study your past and learn from it, but to study what other churches have accomplished and learned, as well. *Breakout Churches* by Thom Rainer showcases churches that suffered through a minimum of five years of decline, then turned the church around for five or more years of growth. There are different denominations and types of churches in the book we can all learn valuable lessons from.

Chapter 10

Starting Over

What would you change about your church if you could start over? If you are replanting or merging on your path to your church's resurrection, then you get the chance to start over and hit the reset button to set a different course for your church. This is a great opportunity to promote health in areas where your church was suffering, physically, emotionally, and spiritually.

Starting Over Physically

When we first moved to Dallas, one of the members came to me and said, "I don't know where to tell you to begin, but may I suggest you start with the by-laws." They were the fourth or fifth generation and had been adjusted a few times, which I am sure is normal to some degree. A few years earlier, changes had been made that were passed with an abnormally low-attended business meeting and current members resented it.

Our by-laws had an abnormally large section on members leaving and what constituted them no longer members. We went to a 501(c) (3) legal documents seminar and streamlined our foundational documents to items needed for business, the IRS, and legalities to protect the church. We went from a 45-page by-law document to 8 pages.

We applied for our own 501(c)(3) for tax exemption status. Then we hired a lawyer to help us with all of our Start-up documents. We showed her the Canyon Creek documents and made these with our future and growth in mind. We leased a property and paid two years of the lease up front, so we could grow into the monthly payment. We hired an architect to help us design our space. Our team took good parts of our last facility, thought about what we wanted our future to look like, and came up with a building plan for our church. We went from a 180,000 sq. ft. building to 32,000 sq. ft. building.

We changed our leadership structure and how we would conduct business. We went from quarterly business meetings to annual meetings. The leaders understood this opportunity to update and streamline, so we took our time and made the changes that would set us up for our future. We were able to analyze and make changes to our new church, under our new structure, with no resistance.

Starting Over Emotionally

There is an unhealthy practice that has permeated into evangelical churches from the Catholic church, where a pastor becomes a caregiver like a parish pastor would. When I went back and read that sentence it sounded very cold towards the people that God has called us to shepherd, but that's just the point isn't it? In all three of the churches, we have loved and had the privilege of leading, there was an expectation of pastoral care that went beyond what would be capable for a growing church. I think this expectation is the beginning of the end of a church's emotional death, because it marks the time a church has turned to be inward-focused and not community-focused.

Please don't misunderstand, I am not against care. Care is an important value that churches must demonstrate. Frankly, the expectation of care in all three of the churches we have led was put in place by former pastors. The pastors wanted to create a co-dependent relationship with the people, by swooping in as a hero and saving the day. This is a demonstration of insecurity and displays a messianic complex, as pastors say to "their people" you need me!

We were blessed with a great staff in all three of our churches and we organized our hospital visits within the daily responsibilities of each pastor. We then trained our deacons to *be* deacons and be there to care for people during difficult illnesses and emergencies. The message we wanted to send our congregation was that Jesus cares for you and so does our church. The message many send is "I care for you, and so does Jesus."

This section may make you think this is a hot topic for me, but it actually reveals deeper emotional issues in the church. There are times I "break protocol" and make the hospital visit when it is not my day if it's a serious illness or an accident.

I can remember getting a call in Jacksonville, Florida from a family whose child had sprained her ankle in a cheerleading competition and called in a panic telling me to meet them at the hospital because their daughter had an accident. I was with a new family who recently visited our church. When the mother told me what was wrong, I asked her if she was in immediate danger, and asked if they need transportation help or help with her other kids. She said, no, we need you here to pray for her. I told her we loved her girl and we would be praying, we would put the request on the church prayer Facebook page, and that I would call her after our appointment and check in. I again assured her we could send some support to her home or hospital. She said goodbye, very disappointed. This was not her fault, it was part of an inward-focused, emotionally sick culture we needed to grow our church away from.

I recently talked to our LIFE Group about principles of healthy growth for our church. I told them in order for us to grow healthy we needed a pipeline of leaders ready to step up and become group and volunteer leaders. I told them that if we only had a support system of paid staff, our growth would be limited. This is a huge issue in the current church culture in our community. We live in a region where jobs are plenty, and life is good. Many people in our region pay for every convenience or need in their lives. In most of our neighborhood, people have landscapers, have house cleaners, go to the car wash, and lots of our neighbors use a company to hang Christmas lights on their homes. There is nothing wrong with any of these things. Our home is in a neighborhood that is median level middle class. The nicer "hoods" are lavish! The point is, people in North Texas pay for services and are not doers. This flowed into the church.

Breaking this habit or culture takes patience and a plan. Today our hospital visitation and care ministry is generated through our LIFE Groups. The first point of contact for an emergency need or health need is the LIFE Group that family attends. LIFE Group leaders have been trained to respond by communicating the need to the rest of the group and rallying the troops to minister to that family. If things are life or death, the LIFE Group Leaders call our Family Pastor and we determine need and proper response. We want to minister to everyone in our church, and we want everyone in our church to be ministers. This will break the cycle of an unhealthy co-dependence of the lead pastor to the parishioners.

Starting over physically and emotionally requires training, patience, and willing participants. Be balanced in your training approach. You do not need to over-emphasize the wrong practices, whereas you do need to emphasize the need for greater ministry opportunities, and to paint a picture of a healthy church: the church that takes care of their business well, the church that shares responsibilities in giving and in ministry, the church where the shepherd has the ability to lead, comfort, rebuke, grow, and multiply.

Starting over Spiritually

The most important message in this book will be what I emphasize or say the most. I want to be careful what I am presenting as my takeaway. Churches today can be sick physically and emotionally and survive. They can get help and grow out of dated methods, take better care of the business of the church, and train people to be doers not just hearers of the Word of God. You do this through great leadership training, detailed policy and procedure building, and over-communicating in your worship services and all church communication. Man-made leadership gifts and abilities can lead churches out of the first two areas. What a church is not about to do is revitalize or resurrect a church spiritually with man-driven efforts alone. This work happens through divine intervention.

> *The effective fervent prayer of a righteous man avails much. James 5:16*

> *....this only happens through prayer and fasting. Matthew 17:21*

The power of prayer and fasting.

I don't know if I have *ever* heard a pastor talk about prayer, gasped in surprise, and said, "THIS what I am missing." There are some things you just know as a believer in Christ, especially a pastor or spiritual leader. We believe in the power of prayer, we teach it, but many of us (starting with myself) should be better at practicing it. I teach my church two times a year about prayer, and always refer to an ACTS model of prayer: Adoration, Confession, Thanksgiving, Supplication as outlined in the Lord's Prayer, given to us by Jesus Christ.

The kind of prayers we need to revive our dead church spiritually are prayers of confession for our past sins. We need prayers of humility as we acknowledge to God we cannot do this without Him. We must offer to God prayers begging Him for wisdom and guidance. I don't think there is a one-prayer-formula for this either, and it may take more than prayer, it may mean fasting also. We do not do these spiritual disciplines to invoke God's power (which we need) as much as we want to let God know that He has our attention and we need Him to guide us. It is an act of submission. God, we cannot do this without you, teach us and guide us to lead and to be the church that YOU have called us to be.

Seek Proper Spiritual Counsel

Many churches in dire need of help, are too small to hire a consultant. One personal goal that I have is for God to use this book to help other churches in their journey of revitalization or resurrection, as an outreach ministry of our church. I am thankful for the amazing family, brothers, and friends that have walked through our journey with us. The advice, encouragement, prayers, resource help, and personal support have made a difference in my life and the lives of our churches.

Pastor Anthony Milas is my pastor and closest brother in ministry. He pastors Granite United Church in Salem, New Hampshire. We have been very close since we were 14 years old. I have served under him as a youth counselor, beside him on a church staff, and far away as we both lead ministries in different parts of the world. We get together three or four times a year, speak for each other, talk two or three times a week, and text almost daily. We pray for, encourage, celebrate our families, and share life together. He is usually my first call with every professional and pastoral decision I have made in my life, and he is a friend who has stuck closer than a brother.

I am also thankful for and blessed by my best friend since the day he was born (1 year and 17 days after me), Joseph Trinkle. He is my accountability partner, financial advisor, and go-to guy. He has helped us physically when our unhealthy churches could not pay us, loved my kids like they were his own. One of the best weekends of my life (apart from wife and children moments) was with him traveling to Minnesota to see our beloved Philadelphia Eagles win Super Bowl 52. We prayed, went to a great church, took communion together, talked about our wives, children and future goals. Watching the Eagles win was a moment we will never forget, but it pales in comparison to the depths of our lifetime of doing life together. My brother is one of the most significant relationships in my life.

I am blessed beyond my ability to communicate fully, with four daughters, four sons-in-law, and the five best grandchildren in the world. Kristina and Johnny with little Rosie and Rocky, Katie and Nick with Bowie, Kelsea and Evan with Logan and Torrin, and Emily and Ryan are not only my physical family, but my intimate spiritual family. They have served in our churches, worked for years for me with no salary, and are the most generous givers in our church. They reflect their mother's beauty and character, and they remind me, daily, why I need them as much as they still need us.

The most significant spiritual relationship in my life is that with my wife, Kimberly. We met in high school, married young, and started our ministry journey together in our 7th year of marriage with two babies. She has followed me around the world, celebrated with me the highest of high moments, and stood by me when things seemed like they were going to crash and burn. She is my absolute #1 best friend, my confidant, my lover, and the perfect woman to share my life with. Our marriage is healthy physically, emotionally, and spiritually. I know that apart from Christ Jesus, I could do nothing. I also know, without Kim, I would not have been able to live through what we have lived through and still have a fresh love for serving the Lord. I promise before the Lord, and I am very aware that the greatest gift in my life, spiritually second only to salvation, is my beautiful wife Kim. This imperfect man could not have found a more perfect mate.

I have worked with some of the best leaders, who believed the work we were called to do was a holy calling for His church; ministry brothers Bruce O'Neal, Tim Chambers, Brennan and MJ Doyle; loyal, trusting pastoral staff like Rowie Suyat, MaBeth Jose, Wesley Beacham, Melissa Tucker, Matt Tucker and Cindy Tucker, Joe Verdecchio, and the best Executive Pastor a church could have, Maryann Stuart. I have served with some godly board members who trusted me and stood by me and trusted me more than I have deserved: David Penland, David Penland Jr, Tim Cosgrove, Matthew Ward, David Schwake, Frank Evans, John Bullock, Kennon Grose, Richard Pascuzzi, David Foster, and Dr. Brian Hooten. The problem is when you start to mention names, you don't want to forget anyone. I am grateful for my mom who made me go to church when I did not want to, for my dad who taught me a work ethic and how to love people. I am grateful for Pastor John Cartright and Pastor Mike Peper who helped me grow up spiritually.

This is not an Academy Awards or end-of-life accomplishments speech. I am emphasizing the incredible spiritual relationships with which God has blessed me. These and many more have kept me close, prayed for me, encouraged and stood by me. The Bible teaches us from Genesis One to the end of Revelation that man was not meant to do life alone. I am glad that I have never faced that. I have a least a dozen people in my life today that surround me with prayer and would be at my side on a moment's notice. We have to surround ourselves with people we can lean on and trust to give us the right answer, not just the easy answer. We need people who will tell us to be careful when our pride urges us to believe the press clippings. We need brothers who will value our marriage and family and stand next to us to keep us from making a bad decision. We also need people who will pick us back up if we have fallen.

Trust the Process

This phrase has been made famous in the sports world by the Philadelphia 76ers. "The Process" is the plan the 76ers had to dismantle the team and the path they were on and go in an entirely different direction. "The Process" started in 2013, when they started trading star players for draft picks. They hired a new coach and drafted potential stars to build their team. They drafted Joel Embiid, Ben Simmons, and Markelle Fultz, and are now looking to add some star power to build their team to potential championship contender. This was mocked by many, but they stuck to the process and are now one of the powerhouse teams in the NBA. When they do press releases of trades or roster moves they use a hashtag #TrustTheProcess on social media.

When you get prayed up, planned up, and prepared to launch your plan you can expect some things. You will experience early excitement from people who trust you and are all in. You will also experience resistance because most people fear change. You need to be prepared for people to leave your church for myriad of reasons. No matter what challenges come with your holy anointing to revitalize or resurrect your church, TRUST THE PROCESS.

One story from the Bible I have claimed and shared with our churches and leaders is the story of Elijah at Mt. Carmel. He challenged the 450 prophets of Baal to a duel, to see whose God would burn their sacrifice first. He gave the prophets of Baal *all day* and dry wood, mockingly encouraging them to call out louder to Baal as they shouted, and danced, and even cut themselves in desperation, trying to get a response from Baal. Finally, as the sun was going down, Elijah soaked his sacrifice and the wood with water, even filling the trench around the altar with water, just as an extra poke in the eye to Baal. Then he stepped forward and called, once, for the Lord to show that He was God. And God rained fire down from heaven, burnt up Elijah's sacrifice, the wood, and the water. Then he had all of the prophets of Baal put to death. He won a HUGE victory.

And the *very next day* he was hungry and weary in the desert where he had run when that nasty Queen Jezebel swore to kill him for what he'd done, scared and wanting to die.

God is taking us through a lifelong process of becoming more like Him. He never promised prosperity, He promised provision. He never promised it would be easy, but He did promise we would not do it alone. People (like Jezebel) will talk bad about us and even threaten us, but we need to trust the process that God is taking us through. We need to trust the process through which God is taking us. If it took 15-20 years to mess your church up, it will take more than a couple days, or even one big victory, to get it back on track.

So whatever process you take your church through, it needs to be communicated, repeated, tweaked, remembered, and celebrated! If you are 100% sure that you are following God's plan for change or life in your church, you can be 100% sure that God has a plan for HIM to be glorified, and the church will experience a win! We communicated our process verbally, through our website, social media, banners, and letters mailed to members. We reviewed, updated, and celebrated. We made sure to constantly affirm those committed, and had many meetings ushering people out the back door. The process was known, so the victories were also. We prayed expectantly. There is no doubt you will experience highs and lows, but God is not slack concerning His promises!

The battle is spiritual because the soul of the church and its health is a spiritual matter. You will be weary, under attack, and doubt your calling. Protect yourself from doubting the ONE who called you and what HE called you and your church to do!

Chapter 11

The Before and After Pictures

I have undergone a personal health transformation paralleling the transformation that our church has gone through in Dallas, Texas. During our first year in Dallas I suffered from a heart attack. My left anterior descending artery was 100% blocked. This heart attack is called a widow maker because without immediate care it has a 70% likelihood of being fatal. I was very fortunate to live 5 minutes from one of the best heart hospitals in the United States, Baylor Heart Hospital. We went to the ER, and I was operated on within 10 minutes of my arrival. I am extremely grateful that God gave me more time, that my wife took me to the right place, and for the excellent care that I received.

After the heart attack, I started a process that was a radical change in lifestyle. For 18 months I went to 3 doctors regularly: a heart doctor, a diabetes (kidney) doctor, and my regular physician. I was on 9 medications, getting 5 shots of insulin daily, and I was not healthy. I met Dr. Brian Hooten, chiropractor and wellness doctor, who helped me put a plan together for me to get healthy. Proper nutrition and exercise helped me to lose 80 pounds in 10 months. I was able to go off my heart meds and am a living testimony that Type 2 Diabetes can be controlled without medication with diet and exercise. My wife has lost 50 pounds in the process, and we are working together to stay healthy for our kids, grandkids, and our church. I am ashamed to say I was a poor steward of my temple and am thankful for this opportunity to do better.

Facebook had an initiative for their 10th anniversary for its members to put up a current picture of themselves, alongside of a picture from 10 years ago. They called this the "10 Year Challenge." My wife is pretty engaged in social media, so she did it, then took my phone and did it on my behalf. Our "10 Year Challenge" pictures look more like before and after pictures from "The Biggest Loser." We both look healthier, thinner, and somewhat younger in the after version. This made me think about our journey as Warehouse Church. Our before picture of Canyon Creek Church in 2015 and the after picture of Warehouse Church today look significantly different.

Before pictures reveal unhealthy characteristics in an unhealthy church

Our before pictures of Canyon Creek Church reveal the church in an extensive period of decline. The attendance had dropped significantly year by year for over 13 years. The church had suffered a prolonged period of apathy and was going through significant conflict regarding direction. The church had a reputation in the community tied into the very public moral failure of the lead pastor 13 years before. The only new families that joined were connected to the school hires. There were limited visitors and occasional new members, but there were more people leaving than staying.

The deacons removed a pastor trying to solve the apathy issue and brought in a wolf in sheep clothing. It took three votes to call this pastor and it demoralized the church. When this pastor's immoral past caught up with him, the board quietly sent him away and the church received its last death blow. The members were so ashamed of the state of the church their conversations revolved around glory days, the only good times they could remember. This is not the first time I am talking about this, but to give an accurate before picture, this was the state of Canyon Creek Church when we arrived in 2015.

The diet, health changes, and process we put together would take us some time. Every church is unique. Your church may have gone through similar challenges, but your church has a unique history, culture, and demographic. When we were being interviewed for Canyon Creek, I was asked ten different ways, "How can we turn this around?" They wanted it to happen immediately, but it would take some time to prepare our plan. You really can't move forward until you get an accurate picture of where you are. Your GPS needs an address of origination and a final destination address in order to give you the proper directions. We could diagnose some of the obvious health issues the church had, but there was no way to put the full plan together until we were able to get our "before" picture in detail.

The scale does not lie

I have a personal routine I go through before I jump onto—excuse me—delicately step onto the scale. I get up, exercise, take a hot shower to burn off that last ounce, dry off completely, exhale vigorously, then take that delicate step onto my friend that day, or maybe my enemy, depending on what it says to me. When I hit new weight loss levels, I am jubilant. When I go a week or so without dropping, or maybe gaining a little, the scale becomes my enemy because it does not lie.

Whatever state you see your church is in, that is where your journey will begin and, unfortunately, that first flashing number is telling, it's brutal, it does not care about your feelings, and it does not hesitate in its response. My nasty number from that mean ol' scale was 348 pounds. I never did anything wrong to her, but she hurt my feelings that day! When you really get to the place where your entire physical, emotional, and spiritual sicknesses are totally exposed, it's hard. This may hurt and even put you in a state of disbelief, but you need the truth before you can put your plan together. You need to know where you are before you can put your plan together of where you need to be.

This took us 18 months at Canyon Creek, 12 months in Philly, at which both churches were spiritually dead, and 2 years in Jacksonville, Florida, our church that was physically and emotional sick. This was not how long it took us to turn things around, this is how long it took us to put our plan together. When you know where to start, you can chart your course.

Drivers, start your engines!

That step on the scale, or, for your church, that financial report and the health diagnosis, reveals what needs to be corrected, and gives you a starting point. So, let's start! The plan you will put together will be comprehensive and cover the three areas of health we have been breaking down: physical, emotional, and spiritual. Your leaders have figured out exactly where you are, and you have systematically put a plan together, that is not easy or a quick fix, and it is time to move forward.

You are performing for an audience of ONE, and not everyone will be happy.

If an ounce of prevention is worth a pound of cure, let's be prepared for some things that will probably happen in your church. Moses led two million Israelites out of Egypt, who were very reluctant followers. They doubted, questioned, and disobeyed. Moses did not win a popularity contest, but he obeyed God (which made him very popular after he was dead, if that's any comfort).

Be very aware of the limitations and boundaries of your by-laws. It is important to do your homework and have the support of your leaders. The days of unanimous votes are behind you. If you have the support of your key leaders and you are prepared for your meetings you will be able to lead through these important meetings

Do not read anonymous letters or emails.

Antagonists and cowards want opinions without accountability or confrontation. Their mode of operating is to lob grenades and run away. Their intention is to hurt and disrespect and CONTROL.

Your leaders must be prepared for people to leave, and be ok with it.

This is easier said than done. When we were in the thick of the building sale at Canyon Creek, we had eight weeks in a row when people met me at the door on their way out of church to tell me they were leaving the church. They even gave us the cliché line, "It's not you, it's us!"

Give extra attention, love, and grace to those who stay with you.

The sale and transition from Canyon Creek to Warehouse Church spanned a period of eight months. We were careful to be very in-the-moment and give extra care during this time. We coached our Life Groups to have some fun activities. We had a summer full of fun Wednesday nights to start the process of rebuilding community into our church. During our first month, our weekly attendance average was 94. The second month we averaged 124.

Over-communicate successful steps and wins.

When (and if) the mass exodus happens and critics get loud or negative social media peaks, you need to remind your people of your big "WHY!" Celebrate salvations, growth, and financial wins. Thank your faithful givers from the pulpit, in letters, and publicly! Be careful not to inflate the story or stats, but when things get tough, your people need to hear from you and your leaders that everything is moving according to the plan. Remind your key leaders to leak good news and positive multi-level communication. Iterate and reiterate your determination to please God, not man, and your commitment to Him.

It took more than a day to put your plan together, be patient.

The steps of a righteous man are ordered by the Lord, Psalm 37:23. Take steps, and be intentional about the steps you are making. Use that GPS idea and know your route and realize it's going to take some time. Set goals, short term and long term, and make sure that, no matter how fast or slow you need to move, that you are moving.

It is ok to make course corrections, and even apologize if you move backwards.

When you start to move and you hit blocks that are out of your control, it is ok to talk about it. Make sure you're the voice of calm and reason and leadership. If you and your leaders are not panicking, your people will be fine. You are not just rebuilding a church, you are rebuilding trust.

Stay close to the Lord, you will need His guidance and love.

Sometimes it may feel like HE is the only one on your side. If you are obeying and following HIS plan. He will never leave you or forsake you.

The before pictures may look discouraging, but when you are in the process, you will notice some wins, even little ones, will start making a difference. The scale will start to creep down, figuratively of course, and each little win will sustain you during tough times. The after pictures will amaze you.

Health feels good and looks good.

When you hit some of your major goals, you will start to pick up some momentum and growth. We have to understand that this is not based on our feelings or because of our feelings. Let us consider what health is going to start looking like for your church.

Healthy churches have healthy members.

Thom Rainer's book, *I Am A Church Member*, gives six characteristics of healthy church members. Your church does not need to be running thousands of people to be healthy. The picture of a "healthy body" comes from a healthy body.

I will be a functioning church member.

We understand our role in the church, as part of the whole body and understand we are part of something much bigger than ourselves. We celebrate our diversity and exist under the banner of unconditional love.

I will be a unifying church member.

One of the unhealthy marks in a dysfunctional church is disunity, therefore a healthy church has a spirit of unity in its members. We value two very important principles to protect unity: gossip and negative talk is not practiced, and there is a spirit of forgiveness and unity. Jesus instituted communion to help cultivate this in our churches today.

I will not let my church be about my preferences and desires.

We are a part of a body that requires us to serve and not have opinions about everything. Our conversations protect the unity of the body. When we want to talk about things in the church, we go to the leaders rather than gossip.

I will pray for my church leaders.

The best person to talk to about our pastor is his boss, God Almighty, in our prayers. We pray for his wisdom in leading, his family, his stamina, and his health. We pray for his walk with the Lord and for protection. And we pray that God will use us to be an encouragement to his entire family.

I will lead my family to be healthy church members.

When our spouses and children hear us talk about the church, it is positive and supportive of the leadership. We support the ministries of the church with our participation. Healthy church members attend faithfully, serve whole-heartedly, and give sacrificially.

I will treasure my church membership as a gift.

Gifts are costly to the giver, and should be honored and appreciated by the receiver. Jesus put this in place so that He would have a presence on the earth and we have the honor of representing Him. We are blessed to carry His name.

The after pictures will reveal significant "weight loss"

If you are carrying too much weight, you are going to look older than your age, be unhappy about your appearance and your health, and feel burdened by carrying it around. When we carry a spiritual weight, like sin or brokenness, we will be an unhealthy body. When we shed that weight, the body of Christ, the local New Testament Church will not only appear to be healthy, it will actually be significantly heathier. We need to *"set aside the weight that keeps us down."* Hebrews 12:1.

When we meet with our leaders every week, we intentionally talk about signs of life that are not reflected by the attendance numbers. We do not do this to take away from tracking growth. I had a professor in school tell us that numbers do not tell the whole story, but winners do keep score. Weight loss, spiritually, is that post-conversion peace all believers understand. We have been carrying the burden of generational sin—and it's gone! We have had the honor of making last payments on large mortgages and loans. The ceremonial burning of that mortgage symbolizes the burden that has been lifted from that body!

Maintaining health is a lifetime journey.

There is a documentary on TV about the winners of the Biggest Loser who have put the weight back on and are living an unhealthy lifestyle once more. They said this is true with a majority of the contestants. The "weight loss" and drastic change in spiritual health habits cannot be a fad diet; it must be a radical life change that is now part of the life of your church. You have to diligently protect this.

In order for me to stay off diabetes medicine, I have to maintain the same low-to-no-carbs diet and absolutely no sugar. If I digress, I will have to go back on insulin. My eating habits are not this week's project, it is an integral part of my daily life, who I am today. When your church adapts healthy practices, make them non-negotiable.

When we started Warehouse Church, we put the old church behind us. We thanked the Lord for it, and honored it properly, but Canyon Creek was not going to be our standard anymore. We made a commitment to long-term spiritual health and, by God's grace, we are not going to stop. In the book, *Nine Marks of a Healthy Church* by Mark Devers, the author shares nine health markers of a healthy church body: Solid Preaching, Biblical Theology, Clear Presentation, Value of the Gospel, Biblical Conversions, Evangelism, Membership Plan, Church Discipline, and Biblical Discipleship. The great part of this teaching is that health is not always synonymous to the statistics. The value of numbers, offering totals, and typical church reports speaks into some of the health, but not the spiritual health as a whole.

We did a series in the beginning of 2018 called "Revitalizing Your Life." We talked about the three areas of church health we have been discussing throughout this book. We are so fortunate to live in the New Testament age of grace, but I love parallel teaching from the Old Testament. Doing so helps us understand God's Sovereignty, and His expectation of exclusivity with our relationship with Him. Moses gave us the Ten Commandments in Exodus 20, and simply states with commandment number one, *You shall have no other Gods before me.* The God of the Old Testament Who ferociously pursued His People, is the God Who gave us His Son Jesus Christ and the idea of a local visible body here on earth.

Thus all the work that Solomon wrought for the house of Jehovah was finished. And Solomon brought in the things that David his father had dedicated, even the silver, and the gold, and all the vessels, and put them in the treasuries of the house of God. 2 Chronicles 5:1 (ASV)

...so that the priests could not stand to minister by reason of the cloud: for the glory of Jehovah filled the house of God. 2 Chronicles 5:14 (ASV)

Simply stated, God's Temple was His dwelling place here on the earth, He made it very valuable, He wanted it to be very detailed, and He had every piece made with order and purpose.

Do you not know that your body is a temple of the Holy Spirit within you, whom you have from God? You are not your own, for you were bought with a price. So glorify God in your body. 1 Corinthians 6:19-20 (ESV)

In the New Testament, the Bible teaches us that we are His Temple, His dwelling place. We are valuable, detailed, and have order and purpose. Consider what He says about the church now:

"You are the body of Christ, and each one of you is a part of it." 1 Corinthians 12:27

We have a tremendous responsibility to take care of the body, the bride of Christ. A healthy Church is not a desire that God has for His Church, it is an expectation and a command. We cannot let His bride be unhealthy. If the task ahead seems overwhelming, there is help.

Chapter 12

What Does HELP Really Look Like?

When is the right time for a church to seek help? This seems like a rhetorical question. If you consider the times in your life you have needed help personally, at one level or another we always need some kind of help. There is an old Chinese proverb that many ethnicities claim as their own that states, "If you give a man a fish, you feed him for a day. If you teach a man to fish, you feed him for a lifetime." I remember seeing this saying on a plaque in my barbershop growing up and asking my dad what it meant. He was kidding with me and said, "I have no idea, I don't like fish," before explaining.

The idea of getting help is a pretty broad idea. Whether your church needs physical, emotional, or spiritual help to be healthy, the church health diagnosis is critical. I want to discuss this because sometimes we can ask for the wrong kind of help, receive unsolicited help, or need help and not know what to ask for.

I think it is fair (and ok) to say that the church receives a lot of requests for help. We consistently have people ask our church for financial help, spiritual guidance, marriage counseling, other forms of counseling, and even help with moving. I'll use the moving help request as an example. Student pastors could start a successful stream of income for fundraising by charging people to help them move. At this stage of my life, I would rather chip in for a mover than ever help anyone move again. That probably sounds a little harsh, and it speaks into the number of times that I have personally helped people move.

Years ago when I was a student pastor, I had a friend in our Philadelphia church ask us to help his family move. I learned so much from this experience relating to future requests. We got to our friend's house, walked in the front door—and their house was a disaster. They did not do a single thing to prepare for our arrival, because their actual desire was for us to do the whole thing. We spent the next 12 hours packing boxes, taking apart furniture, packing closets, organizing, and cleaning before we put one item into the truck. We drove the truck to the new location, unloaded the truck and put everything away. (Did I mention we needed to do some cleaning in the new location before we put the house together?) The family we helped was either super lazy or clueless. I kept telling myself it was the latter, but I have my suspicions! We went to their house a few weeks later and the house we had helped move and put together was a disaster yet again. This family did not need help moving, they needed help learning how to be responsible adults. The church does so many wonderful things for people to help them, but sometimes the help requested is not the help that is really needed.

I remember a young couple who asked me to give them some marriage counseling. The normal thing happened with a couple in conflict. They each came in with a laundry list of what was wrong with their marriage, and what was wrong with their mate. After 30 minutes of this, I asked each of them to share with me what they thought *they* brought into the conflict personally. They shared limited things with me, of course. The wife was very broken, and the husband did not seem interested in reconciliation or doing work to heal their marriage. The husband asked his wife if he could speak with me privately about some "man" issues and she was happy to do so, thinking it would bring progress.

When she left, he told me we were going at this session wrong because he wanted to end the marriage. He explained that, even though they had been married for fifteen years and had three children, he had met the love of his life. He'd been seeing another woman for almost a year. I asked him if the relationship was physical and he said it was. I said, "Let's bring your wife back in." He asked me to promise not to tell her, and I told him I would not make that promise, and that I would tell his wife.

They were seeking different kinds of help. He did not want to restore his marriage. He came hoping I would help him get a peaceful divorce. She came hoping I would change him. They both had some faults, his definitely worse, but they did not ask for the right kind of help.

The communication of help needed at First Baptist Church in Aston, (our second church) was predominantly asking for help by requesting more money from a depleted congregation. The congregation was tapped out. The seniors of the church had invested some, if not all, of their retirement money. The pleas that used to be about faith turned into pleas layered in guilt. The church did not have a money problem, they had a people problem. The pastor was asking for the wrong thing. I am writing this while examining myself at the same time, because we are raising money to complete our building at Warehouse Church. Money funds vision, but the balance between faith, responsibility, and reality can be delicate at best.

We have helped a church that was requesting assistance with an initiative. When we started asking questions and discovered what the depth of their need was, it was similar to our friend who asked for help moving. The church needed far more help than they realized.

The request for help may be as critical as waving the white flag of surrender, and since they were tapped out, they said, "I have all I can take, and I can't take it anymore!" The good thing about this appeal is that it is honest; and the challenging part is getting them to realize what level of help is really needed. It is not wrong to ask your congregation for money for the vision to which they have committed. When pastors over-emphasize money needs, it can potentially push them away. Church leaders, are we asking our congregations for the right thing? Are we asking consultants, businessmen, and strategic leaders for the right thing? Here is a bigger universal question to consider: are we asking God for the right thing? Does the physical or emotional need reveal a spiritual issue in your life or church? It is a fallback answer to say "the Lord knows all, He knows our needs, and He knows what I mean when I say that." The harsh analysis of that prayer is that it is lazy. When James 5:16 tells us, "*our effective fervent prayers mean a lot,*" and Philippians 4:6 tells us to, "*let your requests be made known to God,*" God wants us to be specific and sincere. He desires an authentic relationship with us and wants us to depend on Him.

What should we be asking God for?

Forgiveness	1 John 1:9
Protection	1 Corinthians 10:13
Wisdom	James 1:5
Provision	Philippians 4:19
Vision	Proverbs 3:5-6
Laborers	Matthew 9:38
Harvest	Luke 10:2
Favor	Psalm 5:12

When asking, remember what Peter instructed us to do in 1 Peter 5:7: *Casting all your cares upon Him because He cares for you.*

Malachi 3:10 instructs us to be faithful and obedient in our giving, and then God tells us to test Him to prove His faithfulness. Ask Him for the right thing and watch what He will do in you and your church.

But that's not what I asked for!

The Rolling Stones have a song that starts off with a children's choir singing, "You Can't Always Get What You Want." Did you ever get a bad Christmas or birthday present? I'll answer for you; "Yes, of course." From a human perspective, the church is a place that should be diverse culturally but is usually diverse in opinions. Some of my most interesting confrontations with people have taken place in business meetings. I once passed out an agenda in a business meeting with a header on top that read, "The Good, The Bad, and The Ugly." This was a financial report with some vision pieces of taking our church from barely surviving to thriving. After a few harsh statements from the crowd, I shut down the questions and said that my report was supposed to be called the good, the bad and the ugly and not your responses!

I talked earlier about antagonists but do not want to dwell there. I believe that most people who give faithfully and sincerely care about the church. People will say things, though, thinking it is helping. Their motives are honorable and compassionate, but their communication is horrible. When pastors and board members go into transitional business meetings with challenging news or initiatives, they need to be prayed up and confessed up. We need to guard our tongues and responses, so that we do not speak in the flesh. I've led three-and four-hour church and school business meetings where I really wanted to react harshly and abruptly to people making ridiculous statements or accusations. Sheep can be stubborn, but shepherds are not always perfect, either.

There are times we pray to God asking for resources, provision, and clarity. We ask Him to increase our faith, draw us closer to Him, and then He does it. The problem with human thinking is that we often feel as though God misunderstood or just did not hear us. One of the greatest human examples giving us a glimpse of the mind of God is the privilege of parenting. Our children do not always view what we do while parenting as love. "I love you," often comes in the form of, "No," or "Not now." Sometimes we even say, "Are you kidding me? No way!!" Our even more maddening answer may be, "When you're ready." It just seems that God loves us like this and more. When we start to comprehend that God is God and we are not, and we see that His ways are higher than our ways, we can begin to understand why He does not always respond to us the way we want, but He will always respond with what we need.

I like the optimistic approach to this statement of God doing Ephesians 3:20-sized work in our lives and in our church: *Now to him who is able to do immeasurably more than all we ask or imagine, according to his power that is at work within us.*

When we pray specifically and expectantly, God does great things! Have you ever seen that and more? Have you ever asked God to grow your church and it grows exponentially? Have you ever asked God for provision and HE gives more than you ask or could expect? Have you thanked Him for the abundance of provision that He has already provided, even when you did not ask, or even really acknowledge?

When Life Church in Philly was looking for a home, we prayed God would put us right where He wanted us. The merge with Marcus Hook was so far beyond what we expected or imagined. We went from renters with one-month expense money in the bank, to property owners with a 60,000 square foot building and two years of budget money in the bank. To say this was beyond our expectations is a comical understatement. This was a flat-out miracle in Jesus' name. When you look at many of the miracles in the gospels, Jesus not only healed physical issues, He gave them a greater gift of forgiveness. The crook on the cross next to Jesus merely acknowledges his own guilt and asked for remembrance after Jesus came into His kingdom. Jesus told him he was going to paradise today, simply because he believed. Sometimes we ask, or don't ask, and we get more than we could imagine!

There are also times when we know we need something, anything, but don't know what to say or pray. Marcus Hook Baptist Church leaders told me they needed help getting people in the doors. They not only did not know how to get people in the doors, but they also did not know what to do with them when they got there. They were so blinded by their history and religious rhetoric, along with an unusual level of inward focus, that they had no idea how to connect with their community. I explained to the people what our church would look like if we brought the community into the doors of this church. We talked about the demographic of the multiple cultures represented in the community. MHBC was predominantly white, and of the 60 people who claimed MHBC as their home church, only three families lived in that same community. I told them that if they wanted black, Hispanic, and younger families to start coming to the church, they would need to learn how to talk to and connect with people with tattoos, bi-racial kids, and people with alternative lifestyles. I told them if they wanted people in their church, they would need to learn how to open the doors first.

I have always had a hard time understanding "hair cut language." Barbers have their own language for certain types of cuts and styles for men's hair. I was so lost in my understanding that, for years, I would simply ask for a buzz cut, which I have come to learn also has many variations. Haircut language is cultural, economically influenced, and regionally executed. I was in Boston and saw a haircut happening that I liked, waited for that barber, and I asked him two questions, "Can you do that to my hair?" and "What do you call it?" Then for assurance, I took the picture afterwards to show my barber when I got back home. When I got my cut 3 weeks later I showed Ciarra, my barber, the style and she said it is a "Bald around the ears high fade, with a hard part and thin it out on the top!" I am now 52 and have learned how to ask for my desired haircut. Sometimes we just don't know how to ask for what we need because we really don't know what that need is.

Does your church need help? Ask for the right kind of help from the Provider. Does your church need help? Get ready for more than you ask for as you follow Him! Does your church need help? Learn how to ask!

You can't always get what you want, you can't always get what you want, you can't always get what you want, but if you try sometimes, you might find, you get what you need. Bishop Mick Jagger. 1969

Chapter 13

Before You Start...If You Leave

Kim and I were 18 years and 10 months of age when we got married in 1985. We met in high school and dated for 2 years before we wed. Next to salvation, it was the best decision I made in my life. I must be honest though, when Kim was walking up the aisle, I was scared, and as beautiful as she was that day (and even more today), as she got closer and closer, I got even more scared.

Does anyone really know what they are getting into when they get married?

I had no idea we would have the four most amazing girls and the life we have today. It wasn't easy for her either, that day, I am sure. She had no idea I would leave my dad's business that we thought I'd spend my life building, to move to Missouri, which would be one of our 8 major moves out of 23 different apartments and houses. Our life has been a great adventure. The ministry journey has given us such a rich life. With every move we made and each ministry the Lord led us to, we had hopes, dreams, and expectations, but you never really know what you are getting into completely when you start a new job or ministry. This happened in the three churches we have pastored. The board was not dishonest. We read the financials and took the pulse of the church, but until we jumped in with both feet, we really didn't imagine what the Lord wanted to do through us. The revitalization and resurrection stories of our three churches are not about mistakes anyone made, or how badly or unfairly anyone was treated. The stories are about the new life, health restored, and the lives impacted, before and after.

I wish that there was an easy formula for leaving a church, as well as the best way to get started at a new position. The only real perfect way is to follow the Lord's lead on the way in and follow His plan on the way out. Psalm 37:23 tells us, *the steps of a righteous man are ordered by the Lord*. If we read and submit to the word of God, HE will guide our long term and short-term steps in our lives.

Your word is a lamp to my feet and a light to my path. Psalm 119:105

I have started a new ministry and left ministries I love and people we have loved like family. Leaving both churches was very hard. I am blessed it was hard and not an escape plan or that we were run out of town. We have been blessed to visit and speak at University Church in Jacksonville, Florida and The Bridge Church, just south of Philadelphia, Pennsylvania.

Before you start

I think it would be very appropriate to tell you that you need to be prepared physically, emotionally, and spiritually for your new assignment. Before you jump out with a bigger-than-life vision and start turning things upside down, it is important you get to know your leaders and as many people in your church as soon as possible. Relationship investing is the beginning of building trust. If you are coming into a volatile or broken situation, use your honeymoon time strategically: get in and get settled. You need to go on a fact-finding information journey, and whatever you do, do not take sides with or against people. Love them all. Be careful not to overcommit and under-deliver. Don't forget that when you candidated, you preached your best message and were more ready for that Sunday than you are many Sundays. The fact is, the people are on display when you candidate, just like you are. They had on their Sunday best as well.

You will have a period of time that will be your professional honeymoon. Schedule individual meetings with your board, and for the first six months, meet monthly. Long term, I would suggest once per quarter, but if the situation has early challenges, you need as much face time with key leaders as possible. Be careful not to make any sweeping changes and meet with your staff weekly. During your first week, meet with the staff individually, start planning on who is staying and who you will need to let go. Make sure you are reading some good books: *Revolution,* by George Barna; *Pastoral Ministry,* by John MacArthur; *Fresh Wind Fresh Fire,* by Jim Cymbala; and for personal growth, read *The Measure of a Man,* by Gene Getz.

I would also try to set up some outside accountability or voice that you can tap into when you feel you are getting pulled two ways. You need to know exactly where the church finances are. I would highly recommend having the church execute an audit from a CPA firm, so you know exactly what the balance sheet looks like, the budget, the bank balances, and your overall debt. Get an idea of the state of the property, look for an easy short term win you can lead the church into, like a work night, for example.

Emotionally, I would want to know where the bodies are buried. I would meet with the seniors to understand the current state of their hurts and hang-ups. They will talk if you hang out with them. I would not stir up trouble, but I would want to hear from some of the staff wives, as well as the deacon's wives. If there is dissention they will know. Get to know the community you are moving into and the neighborhood of the church. Meet and greet the church neighbors.

Once you accept the call and move to your new city, try to talk to the former pastor, or even the one before that. This could be tricky if you're following after a mess up, but it is significant to hear another perspective of the church history. Be careful with whom you make alliances and promises. Assess the quality of the staff, if you inherit one, and determine your keepers and short-term staff. Make sure your by-laws are updated and understood. Schedule a meet and greet with the pastor and his family, and with the church as soon as possible. Let them have access with you directly for a while. Get in before others and stay late, and set some precedent with your work ethic right out of the gate.

Pray like you never have and read your Bible daily. You are going to go through some spiritual warfare soon and you need to be ready. Know your budget so you can get your people (and staff) on the same page. Talk about your plan, little by little, on a weekly basis, as you continue to discover more about the church. Plan your preaching schedule for at least a year in advance and get your church calendar together. Be careful not to talk too much about the former pastor publicly, as you only know what you have been told and your first assignment is to build community morale and trust.

You are going to learn a lot about people during the first few months, and they will learn a lot about you. Be ready to be a little bit of a letdown to the people and vice versa. You are not perfect, neither is the church, and it will not take long for that to be exposed. Patience and commitment are important, as well as some margin for error. YOU need time with your family daily and keep your marriage a priority.

Be careful not to over-communicate the faults of the former pastor. Disappointment stays with the position or office. When you continue to talk about the former pastor's failures, you are teaching your people to do the same with you when you make a mistake. You live where you dwell. If you want the church to move forward with you, then move forward.

Once you put a plan for the future together, communicate and tweak it so you can have your starting point and how you are going to get there, in place. Starting strong does not mean dropping the hammer, but it does mean being in the moment and seeking direction from our Lord. Remember that your start isn't as important as your finish. New pastors have to be careful not to succumb to the temptation of being impatient or impetuous.

If you leave

Leaving happens. It was not what we had in our ministry blueprint when we came out of college. I shared a statistic a few chapters ago about pastors who intentionally have affairs. They do this because the pressure from the church was so overwhelming that they had an affair to intentionally disqualify themselves. Many pastors stay too long because they cannot afford to leave their church due to church and personal finances. Dave Ramsey talks about this in his principles of debt free living. He believes that money issues cause more divorces than infidelity and claims that more people would divorce if they could afford to.

As the pastor, you are a shepherd, and the Lord has made it very obvious to you that He is moving you to a new assignment. (This happened to us twice.) When we left Jacksonville, FL, we were blessed to have an Executive Pastor on our team already that we recommended. He is still the Lead Pastor, over a decade later. We were blessed to be able to do the same thing at The Bridge Church, with our Associate Pastor. When Canyon Creek called, we said no, at first, because we did not want to leave the church in its current place financially. The Bridge was not in financial trouble at all, but the church was not ready financially for a leadership transition. The Lord showed us it was His will and He provided more than we could have asked for to confirm His calling. Better men than I have been called into tougher positions and left better than I could have imagined. Through our experience with our boards and pastors who followed us, here are some things to consider when you leave your church:

If the new ministry you're being led to cannot respect your timeline, decline.

You cannot and should not leave your sheep unattended. You might not be able to be a part of the process, but you can prepare the church, and leaders for what is ahead. If the new church/ministry needs an answer faster than you're able to respond, that may be a good sign for you to reconsider. When I was a teenager and had "an emergency," my dad would say, "Your emergency is not my emergency." I don't think you need to be that blunt, but I would direct them to pray, and you commit to do the same.

I told my close friend in Dallas, Kennon, that I couldn't walk away from The Bridge Church that soon. He asked me how to pray so that we could see if this is from the Lord. I told him what to pray for, and we prayed. God provided, and made the path clear to me, Canyon, and The Bridge Church. The other thing to consider is this, if you leave too quickly, is your former church going to think you are running from something?

Clean up anything that could hurt the church or new pastor.

Years ago, we sold a house and my wife told me that we needed to go back and clean before the closing of the property took place. She didn't want anyone cleaning her dirty house. She wanted the new owners to see it cleaned. This is pretty good advice for leaving a church: leave it clean. You may not be able to leave it debt free or be able to build or finish a big project, but you can leave it clean. I had a pastor friend who suggested that I do an audit on the way into a new ministry, so you know exactly where you are when you start. We did this at Marcus Hook. It's probably not a bad thing to consider getting an audit done on the way out, too.

We had the craziest week of clean up duty before we left University. We had to church-discipline a deacon who'd had a public morale failure, confront a male member about appropriate touch, and fire an employee. Do the new pastor and church a favor, and clean things up before you leave, no matter how messy it is.

I talked about Dave Ramsey in this section. I went through Financial Peace University twice! In one of the lessons he talked about living like no one else, so you can live like no one else. He talked about not feeling trapped by your financial consequences. If it means you stay, then you stay. Do the best that you can not to leave a mess for the next pastor. Don't hurt a future opportunity to be invited back. It's hard to leave, but it is heartbreaking not to be invited back.

Be an advocate for the new pastor.

If you leave a church you have been leading for any prolonged period of time, you are probably leaving people you love, who also love you, and it is hard. The new pastor may be very different from you. That is not a bad thing! When your former members call or contact you, do not become a sounding board, or be their advocate to the new pastor. Be an advocate on behalf of the new pastor to them. When you leave a church, you are handing the shepherd's staff for that flock to the new shepherd. There is something to be said about the way that God transitioned Moses and Aaron from leadership over the children of Israel. He took them up to a mountain and did not let the leaders know where he buried them. Moses spoke into Joshua's calling to the nation and stepped aside. If you get to preach a last sermon before you leave, make everything about your gratitude, and getting behind the new pastor. God honors honor.

Your relationship with former church should be through the new pastor.

I am extremely relational, which has both benefits and challenges. When we left The Bridge Church, we left people we loved, led to Christ, discipled, and been through the trenches with them. When I stepped aside, that relationship needed to be through the new pastor. We stayed away from private messaging, texting, Facebook messenger, and former staff, because of great advice from one of my accountability pastors. I had a former staff member who worked for the new pastor call me and ask advice. I told him I would be glad to help him but would let Pastor Aaron know that we talked. This may sound extreme or paranoid, and we did not totally sever relationships, but we did put some distance between them for a while. When we were in the area and wanted to visit the church, we called the new pastor first out of respect. The reality is harsh, but it is sort of a divorce, and you need to step back and respect the boundaries. The importance was not whether people loved me or Aaron more, but that they love the Lord and His church.

Your family is still your first priority.

Your relationship with your family needs to be your priority in your move, not the new church family. Your new church family needs you and they will communicate that. They will ask to get you as much as they can. But you cannot forget that your first ministry is to your family. I am sure this is not a revelation to you, but we all need to be reminded often that if we fail our primary ministry, our church ministry will fail as well. I learned the hard way. We didn't lose our girls, but I needed to do some recon after our time in Jacksonville. The ministry at university was all-consuming because of the school and overall complexity of the ministry. When I visited the church a year later, Pastor Frank asked me what I would do differently if I could change things. My response came right out: I would not have worked so much and enjoyed my kids more. Most parents carry some level of regret. My wife and I made sure to correct this when we went to Philadelphia, and frankly, as much as my family probably needed more of me, I definitely needed more of them. God's plan for our lives works when we follow it. The other part of that is that your church family needs to see you lead your family well, especially when you follow someone who failed morally.

Learn from the past, but communicate the hope of the future.

You are not a victim of the former pastor's mistakes. You are called to lead the church out of bondage and into the promised land! He has to live with his mistakes just like you do yours. We have to remember that we are called to share a message of hope. Just like the resurrection story of Lazarus, God is getting ready to use you to do great things so that others will believe. When reminded of mistakes and failures, remember the grace distribution that you have experienced from God. Don't forget about your own mistakes and weaknesses before you open up dialogue about "the old guy." My brother, Pastor

Anthony, reminds me all the time, "Not these guys, Satan." Our retirement plan includes our wives, kids, grandkids, and most of our sons-in-law (read *just kidding* here!)

Your calling is your calling. You are called to be you.

This section may be for me only, or for people who do what I do, or do something unique in ministry. I am blessed with some incredibly successful pastor friends. I am not just talking about Twitter or Facebook friends, but authentic lifelong relationships. I probably have 10 close ministry friends with churches that run into thousands, including one who works for one of the largest churches in the country. We are in the same age bracket: Gen-Xers. My flesh fights jealousy, insecurity, comparison, and even questioning God when I see pastors do better than I do. I fight the "why me" question all of the time. I recently read an article by Carey Niewhof called, "Jealousy, Envy, Insecurity, and The Heart of a Pastor." When we talk about our ministries or hear people talk about their ministries, pastors and missionaries speak this language of comparison extremes, for instance, "I minister in the most unchurched region of the world," and "my church is located in the heroine capital of Texas." Biggest, farthest, largest, and most. We hear these things all the time, we believe it, we compare, then we fall short of what we want others to think of us.

We all must remember this: "We perform" for only ONE. I am happy for my friends who have been called to an extreme place. I am happy for my friends who lead huge churches. I am thrilled and honored God put a burden on my heart, and I am obedient to His call. My feelings about this is my problem, not that of my friends. Nieuwhof shares five disciplines that will kill envy, jealousy, and insecurity:

Be generous with your praise.

Recruit and promote people who are better than you.

Give thanks for who you are instead of lamenting who you are not.

Learn instead of comparing.

Be honest with yourself and God.

These disciplines are good for every human, in whatever capacity of work or being. If you communicate your calling properly, it is being done to honor God's work, His calling, and His name. If you leave, don't apologize, but don't be arrogant. God doesn't need you, He just has a plan for you that is bigger than you. If you leave, see to it there is fruit that remains as well as a good reputation. If you leave, communicate honor to your people, your successor, and your Father in Heaven. When you arrive at your new church, remember your call, and start growing fruit. When you arrive, put the best plan for growth together, love your new family, honor the past of the church, and get them forward-focused, not stuck in the past.

This chapter is dedicated to all of my pastor friends, obeying God's calling and doing His work beyond their own capabilities. I honor the faithful!

Chapter 14

All ABOARD!

On February 4, 2018, I was able to experience something that I'd dreamed of since I was 10 years old. My brother Joe and I attended Super Bowl LII (52) to watch our beloved Philadelphia Eagles beat the New England Patriots. Our father passed the love for our hometown team down to us like it was a birthright, or a family responsibility. Joe and I were trying to count how many Eagles games we'd attended in our lives (over 100, easily). We were standing on the sideline in the end zone, with green zebra striped pants, a story unto itself, and from the waist down we made it onto a picture in Sports Illustrated.

When he and I were 13 and 14 years old, respectively, we watched the Eagles lose to the Oakland Raiders on TV while our dad got to be in the Superdome in New Orleans to watch it in person. Like a frozen moment in time, I remember telling Joe that we would go to the Super Bowl together someday. We watched the NFC Championship game in two different places. I live in Dallas and Joe lives in Houston. With our phones in our hands and computers in our laps, we watched as the game played on. At the end of the third quarter when the game seemed like a win, we reserved airline tickets to Minnesota. It was our time. We had airline tickets five days before we bought the Super Bowl tickets. We were not going to miss this game. Like typical Eagles fans, we were convinced the team needed us there to support them.

We were not alone. It seemed as though 70% of the crowd in Minnesota's football stadium felt the same way. We wore our very best team gear—and every coat we had. It was -15° degrees in Minneapolis and we were in our seats to be there for our beloved "birds." If you are a football fan, you know the outcome of the game. If you are not, you may be wondering where this is going.

During the 2017 campaign, the Eagles had a young quarterback named Carson Wentz. He led the team to an 11-win, 2-loss season, with 3 games remaining. Wentz was an early candidate for the MVP of the league. The unthinkable happened in the second half of a game against the Rams. Wentz was tackled by two defenders coming from each side while scoring a touchdown and received a season ending injury. We were stunned and thought our chance for a Championship was over. Then a tall, lanky, back-up quarterback who wore #9, jogged out to the field. He led the team to a win over the Rams, and over the next six games would do what we thought was impossible. Nick Foles led the Philadelphia Eagles to beat the New England Patriots in Super Bowl LII. The team had a huge need, and he played at an MVP level during the Eagles playoff run. He would become the MVP of Super Bowl LII. His career was all but done in the summer of 2017. He was contemplating retirement, because he was not getting the opportunities he was hoping for, until the Eagles called and signed him as a back-up to Carson Wentz.

Stories like this are inspiring to young athletes everywhere—to be ready for their shot. They remind me of men who stood up when it was their shot to have great influence. The Bible is full of stories of incredible underdogs, and "back-up quarterbacks" who stepped up when it was their time. This chapter is not about Gideon and his 300 soldiers, David and Goliath, Ruth, Queen Esther or the Apostle Paul. This chapter is about some special men who stepped up when it was their turn, the church boards of University Church, First Baptist Church, and Canyon Creek Baptist Church. The idea for revitalization, or resurrection, was birthed in the hearts of many of those men before I was even part of their church conversation. It would be an injustice to the story of these churches not to acknowledge these brave men. For every antagonist I faced in confrontation, there were a handful of men who stood with me saying "keep going; we are doing the right thing." Writing about these stories and looking into the rear-view mirror of my life is a great reminder of God's personal work in my life. I am also reminded of guys who interviewed me for each of these churches who inspired me. I remember breakfast at Cracker Barrel in Jacksonville, Florida with Mike Wright, Dave Penland Sr., and Dave, Jr. These men were asking me questions while stirring my heart, believing their church could do more. I remember a two-hour phone call with David Schwake, talking to me about how we could get the upside-down financial situation in Philadelphia turned around so we could reach people. I met with Tim Cosgrove and Matthew Ward in Philly, assuring me they were in for the long haul if I would "come home." I remember meeting with John Bullock and Don Anthony, who were faithful but weary men in their mid-70s wanting more for Marcus Hook Baptist Church. I am grateful for Kennon Grose who asked me to pray about helping Canyon come back from the dead. What was in my heart was a growing understanding of how to do this with each church.

These men wanted it before I was a part of their journey. They wanted a healthy church. The perspectives were all different. Some wanted their church to get healthy because they wanted their children to have a healthy church to grow up in. Some wanted the church healthy because their teenagers and young adult children were wandering and had lost faith because of church hurt. Some men wanted the change because they saw their time was short and did not want to die before they passed the torch of a healthy church to younger leaders.

I will not share the names of those who made mistakes, bringing these churches to despair, because some represent life-long relationships, and also because this story is not about failure. This story is about new life. Revitalization or resurrection started with them. They were at the front line. They took phone calls from members questioning them and doubting the plan. They stood strong against antagonists, doubters, and haters. These men stood strong when some of their lifelong friends left the church in disapproval.

I have thought about what it felt like for Nick Foles to run out onto the field, from the sideline to the huddle, right after Wentz was taken into the locker room, and when he looked into the eyes of his linemen or in the stands to see the disappointment of the fans. They were not mad at him, just sad because of their perception of the fate of their season. Something started with *him* that moved his offense, that moved his team and coaches, that moved the city of Philadelphia, and moved my brother and I to Minneapolis during the coldest week of 2017, only to secure the Super Bowl trophy.

The deacons and board members who called, guided, stood by, encouraged, and protected me are the best teammates a pastor could desire. Most were there before, during, and after the revitalization of their ministry. We cheer for some from afar as they continue in their journey with their church. We serve with some today, and I am better for it. We are thankful for church members who followed our leadership and journey. We are thankful for those who left quietly and continue their service to the Lord in other local churches.

We pray for churches and board members all over the world who desire physical, emotional, and spiritual health. Let God plant a dream in your heart and be the healthy church God is calling you to be.

Bibliography

New International Version Bible, Hodder & Stoughton, 2007.

American Standard Version Bible, LuLu Com, 2017.

English Standard Version Bible, Oxford University Press, 2009.

"Death Takes a Holiday'" MASH, Directed by Mike Farrell, 20th Century Foix, 1980. "ER", NBC Broadcasting, 1994-2009.

Shakespeare, William, and Alan Durband. Romeo and Juliet. Hauppage, NY: Barron's, 1985. Print.

Rainer, Thom S., Autopsy of a Deceased Church, Nashville, TN, B&H Publisher Group, 2014.

Dever, Mark, Nine Marks of a Healthy Church, Wheaton, IL, Crossway Pub., 2013

Batterson, Mark, Circle Maker, Zondervan, 2016.

Rainer, Thom S., I Am A Church Member, Nashville, TN, B&H Publisher Group, 2013.

Hauk, Kenneth C., Antagonists in the Church, How to Identify and Deal with Destructive Conflict, Tebunah Ministries, St. Louis, MO, 2013.

Rainer, Thom S., Breakout Churches, Grand Rapids, MI, Zondervan, 2005

Ed Trinkle

For more additional information about this book send questions to: info@advbooks.com

To purchase additional copies of this book, or to see a list of all current titles visit our bookstore website at www.advbookstore.com

Longwood, Florida, USA
"we bring dreams to life"
www.advbookstore.com